HOW TO BE AWESOME AT MARTIAL ART*S*

MATTHEW TEASDALE

First published in Great Britain in 2025

Copyright © Matthew Teasdale

The moral right of the author has been asserted.

Editing, design, typesetting and publishing by UK Book Publishing.

www.ukbookpublishing.com

ISBN: 978-1-917329-91-0

To my wife and family, without you, there is no me.
To my coaches, I have been incredibly privileged to have
such wonderful role models who taught me, inspired
me and guided me in martial arts and in life.
To all the crazy, amazing martial artists out there,
thank you for letting me be a part of your tribe.

CONTENTS

Foreword		vii
Introduction		ix
My Journey		xii
1.	Martial Arts	1
2.	What Makes a Style?	6
3.	Why Do You Train?	11
4.	Art	14
5.	Sports	18
6.	Self-defence	24
7.	Functionality	30
8.	Training to Win	33
9.	The Cube	40
10.	Techniques: good, bad or indifferent	50
11.	Five Ways of Attack	56
12.	Five Ways of Defence	72
13.	Centre Line and Cone of Balance	83
14.	A Triangle and a Sandwich	89
15.	Range Bullseye	100
16.	Range Tactics	108
17.	Pressure Spectrum	117
18.	Tennis, Anyone?	129
19.	The Rhythm is Gonna Get You	134
20.	Here Comes The Science Bit	140
21.	Absorb What Is Useful	151
22.	Learning and Development	155
23.	Be A Good Bad Guy	161
24.	Ageing in Martial Arts	168
Conclusion		180
Acknowledgements		181

FOREWORD

By Ron Balicki

I am thrilled to introduce Matt Teasdale's new book, How to Be Awesome at Martial Arts. Matt and I have trained together for over 30 years, and it has been a privilege to witness his transformation from student to teacher, fighter, and mentor. Our journey began in 1994 when I was invited to Edmonton, Canada, to teach a weekend workshop at a local martial arts school. Among the more than 30 attendees was a 15-year-old boy who stood out - Matt. Despite being the tallest person in the room, it was not his height that caught my attention but the way he carried himself. Quiet and kind, he exuded a presence that belied his years, seeming more mature and composed than many adults in attendance.

When we began training, Matt's serious approach to his practice was immediately apparent. His power, grace, and movement were those of someone with decades of experience, yet he was just a teenager. Over the years, I have encountered many with similar potential, but few have displayed the steadfast dedication that Matt embodies - what I call "grit". If there is one quality I would want all my students to have, it is grit. This trait, above all others, allows one to develop strength, timing, endurance, and other essential attributes. Matt's reservoir of grit is immense and unwavering.

Another admirable quality in Matt is his commitment to learning through meticulous note-taking. He has always been diligent about documenting techniques and insights to ensure nothing is forgotten. When he showed me his vision for this book, I was delighted to see his collection of stick-figure illustrations – simple yet effective memory aids that have guided him throughout his martial arts journey. While he may not be a Van Gogh with a pen, these drawings have been invaluable to Matt and now serve to assist you in your martial arts path.

This book is a testament to Matt's dedication and knowledge, offering a well-mapped blueprint of his journey to excellence. For those serious about martial arts, this guide is an invaluable resource. I hope you find as much inspiration and practical wisdom in its pages as I have.

Enjoy the journey,
Ron Balicki

INTRODUCTION

Hi there!

My name is Matthew, and I'm a martial artist...

That's how we start these meetings, right?

My Name is Matthew, and I'm addicted to martial arts. I've been training and teaching them for more than 30 years now, and I still love practising them every day! In fact, I get a bit antsy if I miss training for a couple of days.

Are you like that? I bet you are. We martial artists tend to be a bit obsessive, don't we?! If you are already a martial artist, you know this when a glazed look takes over your family or friends' faces as you explain what a kimura is for the third time. Or maybe you have had to replace more than a few lamps in your house after inadvertently smashing them with spin kicks. Those lamps took an extra beating during lockdown, didn't they?!

If you are a martial artist, your training leaks out into the real world as you spend your day opening and closing doors, turning off lights, lowering toilet seats, shutting cabinets, and moving chairs with kicks, punches, elbows, knees, headbutts, finger jabs, and Judo chops!

If you recognise the blank faces, the smashed furniture and the manipulation of everyday objects, then you are a martial artist, and you are in the right place!

If you aren't a martial artist yet or are just beginning the journey, welcome to the tribe. You have all these amazing things to look forward to!

This book started as a whiteboard. At my school, I always use a whiteboard to write down the concept or idea that I am teaching that day to help my students visualise what I am showing them. Years ago, I started taking pictures of the whiteboards, so I wouldn't forget what I had taught in previous classes. So now I just have hundreds of pictures of whiteboards amongst my holiday pictures and selfies! What to do with all these photos?

This book is the answer! It compiles and explains some of the whiteboards I have doodled on over the years.

This book explains the concepts and ideas I have used to help myself and my students improve their martial arts skills over the past thirty years. Some of the material is mental, and some is physical, but I have included it all because I believe it will help you grow in whatever style you practise.

In this book, I will discuss the who, what, where, why, and when of martial arts. We will examine your goals and whether your training methods match them. We will also examine the cube, the physics of fighting, the I method, and even a little bit about tennis! I will show you the five ways of attack and the five ways of defence. We will be discussing techniques, triangles, rhythm, ageing and sandwiches. I'm also throwing in a whole load of concepts, ideas and training methods that I think will help maximise your training.

I'm gonna warn you now. My stick drawings are rubbish! My students wait every week with bated breath to see what kind of terrible drawings I will come up with. I toyed with having a professional draw the illustrations for my book, but my wife and I didn't feel it would be authentic. If you were training at my school, you would be subjected to my drawings, so I feel you, dear reader, should be subjected to them too! You're welcome!

Of course, I can't take all of the credit here. I stand on the shoulders of all the great martial artists I have learned from. The ideas in this book have been learned, borrowed, accumulated, dusted off, pinched and passed down. Some are even brand-new!

All of the concepts and ideas in this book interlock and overlap, so I apologise in advance if I repeat material or bang on about something too much!

I hope sharing my whiteboards with you will help you find your next level of training. If it helps you understand martial arts or yourself a little bit better, those whiteboards will have all been worthwhile. Thank you for joining me on this journey, I am very excited to have you here!

MY JOURNEY

Growing up in Edmonton, Alberta, Canada, meant I was destined to be a hockey kid. Me and every kid I knew wanted to be Wayne Gretzky. I played hockey from the age of five until I was 12, and I absolutely loved the game. I even loved the six am power skating lessons my mother took me to, although it may not have seemed like it at the time! As well as hockey my parents encouraged me to play every sport I could. I got the chance to participate in soccer, baseball, curling, tennis, squash, racquetball, badminton, table tennis, downhill skiing, cross-country skiing, and even snowshoeing!

After a broken tailbone put my hockey career on hold, I badgered my mother to take me to some sort of martial arts class after my friend Brian became a national karate champion. I was tired of always losing to him in our impromptu basement sparring sessions. She took me to a local tae kwon do class, inadvertently putting me on the path to my lifelong passion and career.

I remember that first class well, as I broke my toe with my very first kick on the heavy bag. I must have loved it, as I kept going back. I can also remember the stretching portion of the class, when my training buddy and I would quote the movie Bloodsport and try to keep our uncontrollable giggling hidden from the instructor!

When I was 15, I was reading a martial arts magazine when I came across an advert that claimed to teach Bruce Lee's martial art, Jeet Kune Do, right there in my hometown! I knew that I had to train there if I wanted to progress.

In addition to Jeet Kune Do, BSM martial arts academy taught Kali, Grappling, Muay Thai, Kickboxing, and Kung Fu.

I was awestruck and thoroughly hooked.

That was also the year of my first trip to Los Angeles for training. Now, remember, I was a naive 15-year-old boy who didn't know how lucky he was! On that first trip, I got to train with Royce Gracie, Rickson Gracie, Larry Hartsell, Paul Vunak, Dan Inosanto, and the person who was to become my primary coach and influence, Ron Balicki. I know, right?! You don't get a much better start in martial arts than that.

By 1997, I had had a few fights in combat sports and had begun working as a door supervisor and security guard.

I can remember my first day as a door supervisor. I was a skinny 18-year-old who was scared to death, but I wanted to "test out" what I had been learning in the gym.

The head doorman told all the new recruits, "This is not Road House, and you are not coolers!" He then pulled me aside and said, "Seeing as you are a martial arts guy, I would like you to be our knife man." GULP. "What does that mean?" I asked. "Well, if anyone pulls a knife in the bar, you get to deal with it."

Yikes. "Get" to deal with it? It's as if it's some kind of reward for being a martial artist! I knew then and there that this was very, very real! Fortunately, at that club, I was never called on to deal with a knife, but the experiences I had on the door over the next six years shaped how I looked at my training and self-defence in particular.

In 1997, I also helped my training partners Dan Rizzuto and Ben Poss open a school in Edmonton, Canada. After a slow start, we all went our separate ways, with me travelling to England to visit my family and spend a year finding myself!

Landing in England gave me a fresh start, but I still had no idea of what I would do or how to go about it. I was living in the relatively small town of Hexham, where my father was born and some of my older family was living. I was on the precipice of having to decide on a career path and stop loafing around for the rest of my life. I had considered a job in forestry in Canada or as a close protection officer in the UK. While these jobs seemed appealing, I still yearned to pursue martial arts further. Fortunately, I met my long-time training partner, Simon English, who was teaching kickboxing at a local leisure centre. We started training everywhere together. Badminton courts, driveways, fields, attics, living rooms, kitchens, staircases, back gardens and even riverbanks in the pitch black. (To which the police were called!)

Simon and I started a class in a local leisure centre, which really piqued my interest in teaching. From 1998 until 2004, I worked as a doorman in a nightclub. This freed my days and early evenings to train and teach as much as possible. I have taught in fields, leisure centres, gyms, school and church halls, and even a railway club! While it wasn't enough to make a living, I felt like this was paying my dues. I got to learn my craft in all these little places with classes of five or six people. It gave me the passion to keep going and push myself to the next step.

I found my home in 2002 when we moved into our current school in Newcastle upon Tyne, UK. We moved into a shell of a building nestled in the budding artistic area of the Ouseburn Valley. It needed a heck of a lot of love, but fortunately, we were surrounded by people who cared about the training and what we were trying to build. They made it all possible.

Since 2004, I have been very fortunate to teach martial arts as a full-time career. I am so proud that we are still in that same building, teaching and training new people every week. We have come a long way since those days, and when I look back on my martial arts journey, it inspires me to help others get started on their journey! Once you start down your path, you never know where you will end up!

Most of my experience comes from Filipino martial arts, Thai martial arts, Silat, Jeet Kune Do, and Shoot Wrestling. So, most of my examples and descriptions will come from them, but all of the principles and concepts in this book will cross over into whatever style you are training in.

This book is all about you. Whether you are training for fun and enjoyment, self-defence, or competition, I hope you find something that helps you improve, grow, and become the best martial artist you can be.

So, from 30 years of rambling in class to setting it down in pen and ink, here is: How to be Awesome at Martial Arts.

Good luck, have fun, and Bahala na!
Matt

Thank you and Good luck!

1. MARTIAL ARTS

Martial arts are splendid and varied. Sometimes, they are chaotic and warlike; sometimes, they are peaceful and calm. They can resemble a tiger, a monkey, a snake, a whirling dervish, or an elegant ballet dancer. They have hard, soft, in-between, and truly out-there styles.

People who train in martial arts do everything from meditation to punching and kicking, to grappling and training with weapons. They smash bricks with their hands and glass with their heads. They jump off buildings and do really weird stuff to their genitals.

Some believe it's a bit of fun with the family at the weekend, and some believe that if they train every day, they will become invincible superhumans. Needless to say, it is an exciting world to live in and be part of!

The more you learn about the wide variety of styles and systems, the more addictive they become. I am constantly astounded by how all cultures have developed some form of martial art at some point. It's interesting to see how these hand-to-hand combat styles evolve even after guns and bombs have made them somewhat obsolete.

For the most part, martial arts were developed during different periods to help one set of people defend against or attack another.

Primitive-age martial arts focused on hand-to-hand combat and weapons fashioned from the materials available in their environment. Wood and rock were converted into clubs, staves, spears, bows, and slings. To repel these new weapons, armour made of leather, cloth, and natural fibres was developed.

Metallic age martial arts added deadly edges to their

weapons, changing warfare forever. Swords, shields, spears, arrowheads, and cast armour brought a whole new element to the clash of combative contestants.

Tribes or armies have developed various battlefield tactics depending on the environment, the enemy, the arsenal, and their attributes. For example, smaller forces with lighter arms used guerrilla tactics to hit and run against a more powerful, well-armed foe, whereas a large, well-trained, and armed force worked together in rank and file to overwhelm an opponent.

The Filipino martial arts of Kali, Eskrima, and Arnis were developed to hit and run the larger and better-equipped Spanish invading forces. In contrast, the Thai weapon art of Krabi Krabong, which was used in line formation, focuses on techniques that would damage the enemy while not injuring your fellow troops who were standing shoulder to shoulder with you.

The constant one-upmanship of weapons and armour kept everyone on the "cutting edge", if you will! (Ba Dum Dum) The razor-sharp edges of warring samurai clans cut through their opponents' wooden armour. In Europe, metal armour required more of a bludgeoning sword or tin opener approach.

Aside from the physical aspects of the martial arts, all of these tribes and armies developed psychological and philosophical methods to deal with the harrowing combat experience. Some styles developed spiritual notions that protected them in battle, like the Filipino warriors who inserted anting stones (amulets) into their bodies and tattoos onto their skin before running towards the American guns with their deadly swords. Here's a bit of trivia for you: the American "leather necks" got their name from the stiff collars they wore to protect them from the rushing swords of the Filipino warriors. Now you know!

Religion played a significant role in combat, as the belief

in a rewarding afterlife helped terrified troops overcome the emotional inertia of entering a situation in which they were highly likely to be killed.

So, what has happened to these arts? Fortunately, they have trickled down, filtered through the hourglass of time, and evolved into something we can all access in our everyday working lives.

Some arts are being preserved just as they were hundreds of years ago. For example, martial artists scour ancient texts and recreate warfare from the times of the battles. Some maintain the arts handed down to them with careful and systematic personal training across the generations. These methods were passed on with the same dedication and pride that one would give a family heirloom to a descendant with the instruction and hope to continue its journey long into the future.

Many modern combat sports evolved from the need to keep a bored and rambunctious army occupied when they weren't in combat. Wrestling, boxing, Pankration, archery, and even darts were good ways of occupying the minds and sating the adrenaline-fuelled bodies of potentially mischievous soldiers.

It's also interesting to see how martial arts travel and evolve across nations. Techniques from the ancient arts of England look remarkably like those in the medieval texts of Europe, which are almost identical to those of the Philippines and other occupied countries. You can trace these journeys through warring countries and imagine how opposing armies would adopt their opponents' effective techniques and tactics and make them their own.

Each art faced a complex evolution through advancements in technology and tactics. Their medieval skirmishing tactics failed against the advancement of the musket and cannon. The ranked approach of the colonial era failed against the appearance of the devastating machine gun on the battlefields of World War I. Like today's modern combat sports, we must evolve to survive under pressure.

It is remarkable that we can today access all of these incredibly effective, killing arts at the touch of a mouse button or the turn of a page.

These arts have travelled through history, across continents, and been plunged into the blood and mud of battlefields.

They have persecuted and invaded rivals, condemning countless to their deaths. They have been used to gain wealth, power and land.

They have also helped the subjugated rise up and strive for a better life for themselves and their children.

They have been used for good and evil, order and chaos, and now they have landed gently in our laps.

And that's just the arts themselves. When we dive into the individual schools, another vast spectrum of martial arts opens up. Each coach, instructor, Sensei, Kru, Guro, and Sifu has their take on martial arts and how they are delivered to their students.

During my time in martial arts, I have seen instructors who teach people for fun and health. I have seen coaches who push their students to the edge of their sporting ability to create the best professional fighters they can.

I have attended schools that focus more on discipline and tradition. These schools run a very tight ship, as the art they teach is an heirloom that has been passed down to them through many generations. I have witnessed military-type training given to businessmen who revel at the chance to disarm a fake AK-47 from the hands of a balaclava-wearing attacker.

I have even encountered clubs that one may regard as cult-like. There is only one way to do things with these guys: their way. They have a tight rein on their students and their actions. If these clubs take a wrong turn, they can sometimes descend into criminal behaviour.

All of these methods have their place and purpose (except criminal behaviour, of course), and they all believe that they are doing the right thing for themselves and their students. As a martial artist, your job is to find the right gym for you and your goals.

I feel very fortunate to have found this thing we call martial arts!

2.   WHAT MAKES A STYLE?

"What's your style?" This is the famous question Bruce Lee's oafish opponent asks him onboard the Chinese junk boat in the movie Enter the Dragon. Bruce, of course, iconically replies, "It's the art of fighting without fighting."

By the way, what happened to that guy? The guy was lured down into the rowboat, and then Bruce gave the tow rope to a group of kids! I don't know how responsible those kids looked. I think Bruce straight-up murdered that guy, or maybe he is still floating around the North China Sea!

Sorry, I digress.

So what makes a style? In theory, the laws of physics apply to all of us equally, and we have fairly similar biology, so how is it possible that we, as a species, have come up with so many different ways of beating each other up?

Culture

Where was your style born? What did society look like at the time your style began? Was it feudal Japan? Was it an Indian tribal community? What were the rules of that society? Maybe only the wealthy and upper class were allowed to practise the art. Maybe only soldiers trained in the style.

If it was a duelling art, what were the rules? What constituted an honourable duel in that society? How did the participants gain "satisfaction", and why?

Did the community's culture dictate certain battlefield etiquette? If specific rules were not followed, would honour not be fulfilled and victory deemed unsound?

It's funny, but there is a strange kind of humanity in having rules for war. These rules will have shaped the style and ethos of your art to this very day.

Attributes

Styles were created by and for the people. The people who performed the art will have considerably influenced how or why the style was developed. This is where the individuality of training becomes essential. Do you suit the art you practise?

Was the art constructed for generally smaller people to defeat a larger enemy, or was it modified to suit one person? The Filipinos have defended their 7640 islands for centuries against larger, better-armed foes. They didn't have the luxury of standing and meeting the invaders in a pitched battle. They had to think outside the box and use hit-and-run tactics to thin the ranks and inspire fear in their enemies.

Bruce Lee spoke about the individualisation of training. Because no two people are the same, his Jeet Kune Do will look different from someone else's. Dan Inosanto had to modify the techniques Bruce Lee showed him because he didn't have the same attributes as Bruce.

Political and economic climate

Some styles were forged in secret due to the hostile occupation of their country at the time. The true fighting spirit was often developed under oppression. Many Filipino, Indonesian, and African styles were practised under the watchful gaze of their occupiers.

These styles were often cleverly practised as dance, and I love the idea that they were performing their seemingly innocent routines to their persecutors, all the while having murderous intentions!

The country's economic climate can be very influential in how its fighting men and women train. It also affects the technology they have available. Weapons, armour, supplies, transport, and food are all vitally important and depend on the region's wealth.

For example, the fighters of Okinawa had to use primitive farming weapons to fight back against the invading samurai, as they didn't have bespoke weapons.

Many invaded nations had to use primitive weapons, but they also had superior tactics and a better knowledge of the landscape they were fighting in.

Environment

The location of combat influences the development of the art. The Indonesian martial art of Harimau Silat was developed to address the low fog that was common in the area at the time. The low stances and ground postures make sense when you can disappear from your enemy below the mist.

Some kung fu styles were developed in tight urban spaces. Large movements and spinning kicks are not tactically sound if you fight in narrow alleyways.

Have you ever watched ice hockey enforcers duke it out? You will see very few kicks or knees, probably because they are illegal! But it's also tricky to maintain good balance on such a slippery surface if you lift your leg off the ground. They also tend to hang on to each other for stability, among other things.

Another developmental factor is replicating something in the martial artists' environment. You will undoubtedly be aware of the proliferation of animal styles in martial arts.

When I see the animal styles in action, I am reminded of the Jean-Claude Van Damme movie The Quest. "Now he's a monkey.... Now he's a snake!" (PS: If you haven't seen the movie The Quest, that's your homework for tonight!)

Human beings are good at replicating things they deem to be successful, and by mimicking animals that have dominated combat, we have introduced some of our most unique movements to the fighting arts. We have monkey, snake, tiger and crane styles. Styles of mythical dragons, golden centipedes and 10,000 bees. Maybe there is even a devastating hamster style out there somewhere!

This replication almost certainly occurred between opposing combatants on the battlefield. Defeated armies will have studied their losses to improve in the future. This concept is well represented in today's combat sports. You win, or you learn.

My wife says I'm a nerd, and she's right because I like to try and get into the mind of a historical martial artist living in their own time and place. It takes some imagination, but how would the place where they lived look? What was their upbringing? How did they come to be in the fight? Some people were born and bred to be part of a fighting group, while some were forced to be there. As they say in acting, what was their motivation?

Another interesting question is: once the art is removed from its original context, is it still functional? If we are in a self-defence situation in a pub, is it necessary to drop to the floor to get under the fog? If we change the training methodology of the particular art to suit a modern environment and enemy, is it still the same art?

What matters to us is that we clearly define our goals to understand why we want to train in martial arts.

3. WHY DO YOU TRAIN?

On the surface, it may seem a very obvious question. My school has a questionnaire for new starters asking why they want to train in martial arts. Over the last 20-plus years, we have had thousands of people through the door, and I would say 95% of them have listed these three answers:

To learn to defend myself.
To get fit.
To build confidence.

That seems very plausible. But underneath the straightforward answers, there are a whole host of amazing benefits we gain from martial arts. One of the cool things about what we do is that the benefits are on a time release. Some things will improve immediately, and some benefits take three, five, ten or even 20 years to show themselves.

It's very important to be clear about why you are training. Matching your goals to your methodology is the first step to becoming awesome at martial arts. We have to figure out if you are in the right place before we properly get started.

On the next page, I'm going to write two lists. The first list is some of the more obvious benefits of training in martial arts. I want you to circle the ones you feel are important to you. This will give you some indication as to what type of martial art you should be leaning towards. The second list will help you decide what sort of school you are looking for. There are many additional reasons beyond those I have mentioned here. If you have any more reasons, please add them to the list.

List one: more obvious benefits.

- **Health**
- **Attribute development**
- **Learning new things**
- **Resilience**
- **Self-defence**
- **Stress reduction**
- **Fitness**
- **Flow state**
- **Building confidence**
- **Competition**
- **Self-discipline**
- **Achievement**

List two: less obvious benefits

- **Belonging**
- **Acceptance**
- **Culture**
- **History**
- **Travel**
- **Inspiration**
- **Coaching**
- **Community**
- **Awareness**
- **Language**
- **Social life**
- **Motivation**
- **Lifestyle**
- **Contribution**

Now that you have selected your reasons for training, you can determine what type of gym is right for you. Most schools teach one style in a very specific manner. You will have to try them out to see if that particular school meets your needs. Some schools offer multiple styles and utilise different teaching methods, which may or may not appeal to you, depending on the variety you desire in your experience.

There are many factors to consider when it comes to selecting a martial arts school. Some of the things to consider are:

- Location
- Accessibility
- Price
- Value
- Schedule
- Facilities
- Atmosphere
- Attitude
- Structure

This is by no means an exhaustive list, but it will give you a basis on which to start. The best thing to do is to travel to the gym you want to try and see if it fits your travel and schedule needs. See if you can sign up for a free trial so you can experience the atmosphere and class structure. Most importantly, how does the whole experience feel to you? If it suits all your training needs, give it a shot!

Remember, your training needs may change over time, and it's perfectly okay to find a new place to train to accommodate those changes.

In the next chapters, we are going to look at the three categories that most schools teach and give you an idea of where you need to be.

4. ART

I divide martial arts training into three categories to help my students understand what the purpose of their training is. All three of these categories have important and admirable goals within them. Knowing your goals and understanding why you are training makes it much easier to know if you are on the right path.

The three categories are:

- **Art**
- **Sport**
- **Self-Defence**

To me, art is subjective. It doesn't matter if it will save your life or if you will win a UFC title with it. You practise the art because it makes you happy. It's something that helps you get through the day. It could be something as simple as moving your body in a way you never have before. It might be interesting to you historically or artistically. And most of all it is fun for you. Paul Vunak defined this as self-perfection. Something that makes you a better person than you were before.

The cool thing about subjective training is that we don't need to pressure test it. It becomes more about performance in a vacuum. It can be technique-led. It is about memorisation, perfection and demonstration of a variety of movements. In training for art's sake, we don't need to focus on taking ourselves out of our comfort zone against a resisting opponent. Art can be practising your kata or forms. It can be shadowboxing or having a workout on a heavy bag. It can also be drilling some weapon techniques with a friend. It can be practising leg locks

on your partner while you are watching a movie. (Of course, that has never happened in my house.)

There are millions of people out there who play tennis just for the sake of it. They don't feel the need to compete, only to play. They love the movement, the social aspect, and the feeling they get after exercising for an hour. For some, it can make exercise more enjoyable than just running on a treadmill. That is the art of tennis. For some, just to play the game is enough.

Tai Chi is a wonderful art that helps millions of people stay fit and mobile, especially in their older years. My grandmother did Tai Chi at her local social club, and she loved it. Although she had no knowledge of martial arts or fighting, it provided something that helped her on a daily basis.

Now, I'm not saying that Tai Chi isn't practical in a fight. That would depend entirely on how you train it, but when it's just about you, how you feel, and your enjoyment of it, it's art.

As well as describing the particular arts we are practising,

I think the words martial arts are a yin-yang coupling. The word martial means power and destruction, ferocity and fire. Art covers the softer side. It's beauty and grace, it's love and water. (That sounds a bit mushy, sorry!)

For years, I struggled with the concept of art. It seemed weak to me. When I was working as a doorman, I thought I couldn't afford to waste my time on things that didn't directly help me fight better. It wasn't until I saw a video with Rick Faye that I realised I was wrong. In this video, he said it is ok to train things that are fun for you. As long as you are training what you need to train at least 51% of the time, you will be fine. That video unlocked me. It gave me permission to do things that I wanted to do even if they weren't directly functional to fighting. What I didn't understand then was that the art side of things is often the reason you stay in martial arts, especially when you are struggling with the martial part.

I really enjoy using the wooden dummy from Wing Chung and JKD. I find it quite relaxing to work through the motions, focusing on form and flow. To me, it's a form of meditation. I have no preconceptions that this will help me defend myself in the here and now; it's purely for my enjoyment. I tell you what, that wooden dummy took a beating during lockdown, and it kept me sane!

I said in the last paragraph that training the art side of things won't generally help me in the here and now. That is true, but what I didn't say was that it will certainly help you in a few years' time. The attributes you learn when training for art are a slow burn, and you won't notice them getting better until you have trained them for ten years or more. This is patient learning. It's very hard to keep doing something if you know you won't see the rewards until a decade down the line, but believe me, it will happen, and it will be worth it. Attributes like coordination, ambidexterity, tactile sensitivity, and flow are hard-won but will help with everything else you train.

Now, here is the catch. You must be very honest about your training. It can be dangerous to train in art and call it sport or self-defence. Our goal has to match our method. If my goal is to have some relaxing training, focusing on movement, the wooden dummy is a good choice. If my goal is to improve at Muay Thai sparring, the dummy would definitely be a bad choice! A general rule of thumb is that if what you are training doesn't include timing, energy, motion and pressure, you are probably training in art.

It takes a great deal of humility to admit that maybe this training won't save your life or help you compete at a higher level. You do this for the fun of it and because you love it. And you know what? That's okay, you do you!

THINGS THAT AN ART-BASED SCHOOL WILL FOCUS ON:

- **Fitness**

- **Movement**

- **Flow**

- **Forms**

- **Techniques**

- **Partner work**

5. SPORTS

The easiest of our three categories to define is sport. We have all watched boxing, K1, Muay Thai, and MMA on TV, so it is pretty clear what a sport is.

There is a huge variety of combat sports out there, from the mainstream to the truly unique and everything in between. I'm sure you created some game as a kid where you and your friends made up a set of rules and tested each other to see who was the best.

Growing up in Canada, we, of course, came up with a hybrid boxing and ice hockey event. Our friends' basements became stadiums and arenas as we took turns putting on our ice hockey helmets and gloves. Now, the rules were you could pummel away till your heart's content with your right hand, but your left hand had to keep hold of your opponent's shirt. If you fell or let go of the shirt, you lost! It probably will never make it to the nightly sports news, but it was big time in our eyes.

Without hyperbole, there are a zillion types of striking, wrestling, weapon and projectile sports to watch. With the advent of the internet, you can spend whole days of your life descending the weird and wonderful rabbit hole of combat sports.

Sports arts usually have a clearly defined set of rules that the players must abide by. To this end, they are usually strategy and attribute-led.

To participate successfully in sports, we need to have very consistent fundamentals. We need to find the correct fighting platform or cube (see Chapter 9) for the game that we are playing. We then need to be able to perform our basics and hold our cube under heavy pressure.

We will also need an excellent knowledge of strategy. I'm a big fan of the adage: unless you are much better than them, don't do what is best for you; do what is worst for them. In MMA, if you are facing a good striker, it may be your best bet to take them to the ground and submit them. It's important to analyse your opponent. What are they good at? What do they struggle with, and how can you exploit that? Nowadays, it's pretty easy to get hold of fight videos of your opponents and study their style to get an idea of what you should be trying to do. But remember that if the video is more than a few months old, the fighters will probably have grown and changed, so you may be planning for a different fighter than the one they are now! A good corner person will be a valuable asset to your in-fight strategy. Between rounds, they will give you sound advice on what you should try to do next.

Fitness is our next challenge. We need to build the majority of our fitness in our primary training. If you are fighting in Muay Thai, you must be hitting pads and sparring most of the time. You can supplement that training with good, solid cardiovascular and strength training.

Without a fantastic fitness base, everything else will go out the window. I found this out in my last fight. I had matched against a much bigger and stronger opponent, and silly me, I didn't take the training very seriously. I had been out partying the weekend before...oops! It was a painful lesson. By the end of the first round, I could barely keep my hands up, let alone think about strategy or throw any meaningful strikes. It's a horrible feeling being in the ring with someone beating you up, and you can do nothing about it.

Fitness is one of many attributes that you will need to perform in competition. We must constantly strive to develop ways to hit harder, move faster and see the opponent's attack earlier. Some attributes that you will need in all combat sports are:

- **Speed**
- **Strength**
- **Power**
- **Explosiveness**
- **Agility**
- **Flexibility**
- **Timing**
- **Spacial relationship (distancing)**
- **Non-telegraphic motion**
- **Awareness**
- **Fight IQ**
- **Durability**
- **Determination**

The list goes on and on. I want you to have a think about your attributes. I have put a chart here for a little exercise in self discovery! Write down the attributes you use the most. In the second column, give yourself a rating between 1 and 10 for that attribute. (Be honest!) In the last column, write down how you will improve that rating. This will help you find out what you need to work on and what you are doing well at.

Another major piece of the puzzle is sports psychology. Remember, strategy is about them, and psychology is about you. I really like the stoic approach to this. The only things we can control are how we think and how we act.

If you haven't read the book *Happy* by Derren Brown, I highly recommend it. Among all of the wonderful insights into life, it provides a wonderful passage about competition. Essentially, what he says is that if you focus on elements you can't control,

Attribute	My rating out of 10	What I can do to improve it

i.e. beating your opponent or how well they are playing, you can create a downward spiral of disappointment, fear and failure if you begin to lose. Alternatively, you can focus on what you can control, i.e. playing the game as well as you can. This way, you aren't failing, even if your opponent is beating you. They are just better than you on that day. You are always able to play the game better when you are more relaxed, focused and free from the negative emotions brought on by perceived failure.

I have trained and cornered fighters who lost the fight in the dressing room before the bout even started because of the incredibly intimidating pressure of winning. Most fighters and sportspeople, including world champions, struggle with mental challenges, so if you do, too, don't worry - you are in good company.

I remember a team of us driving to one of my first fights when I was about 15 years old. It was a seven-hour drive, which gave me a long time to contemplate all the horrible things that would happen to me in the ring.

Fortunately, I was reading Bruce Lee's The Tao of Jeet Kune Do in the back seat when I came across a passage that said, "If you have butterflies in your stomach, it means you are ready. It is when you don't have butterflies that you need to worry." After reading that, I thought, "OK, this is normal; I can do this."

Sportsmanship is also crucial in a competition. I constantly drilled this into my fighters, and I think they had a better experience because of it. Psychologically, playing fairly and acting professionally will make you immune to self-reproach.

I always thought that if you can't win within the rules, you don't deserve to win. Winning outside the rules always leads to self-doubt and the question of whether you are actually good enough to win. Winning outside the rules doesn't mean you beat the person; it just means you beat the system. I preach humility in victory and magnanimity in defeat. Remember, nobody likes a sore winner!

I had a student who got knocked out in the first ten seconds of an MMA fight with a head kick. Amazingly, he got up with a big smile on his face and proceeded to high-five the crowd on the way out of the cage. The audience loved him!

Defeat is not nice, but it's going to happen. Dust yourself off and focus on what you can learn and improve for the next time.

Whether you play for fun or money, remember to play because you love the game!

THINGS THAT A SPORT-BASED SCHOOL WILL FOCUS ON:

- **Fitness**

- **Conditioning**

- **Drilling**

- **Pad work**

- **Sparring**

- **Sparring games**

- **Pressure testing**

6. SELF-DEFENCE

Self-defence seems to be a catch-all definition for anything we do in martial arts, and in a way, that's right. Everything you do in training will undoubtedly supplement your ability to defend yourself. Still, not everything you do will be engineered to increase your capacity to defend yourself as a primary goal.

This is an excellent time to examine the distinction between primary and supplemental training.

Primary training is focused on doing the thing you are trying to do. Supplemental training is all the other bits and pieces that will help us do the primary thing better. Does that make sense? Probably not! Let me explain it better.

Take swimming, for example. I swim about as well as a brick, but I know that to get better at swimming, you will be putting in about 80% of your training time in the pool, swimming in one way or another. This is your primary training.

The other 20% will be used to lift weights, work cardio on the treadmill or train your movement on dry land. This is supplemental training.

Both are necessary, but we must ensure the supplemental training doesn't take over the primary; otherwise, you will only improve at weight lifting, running, and dry-land movement.

That means that in self-defence, we have to spend 80% of our time working on self-defence skills, such as the interview (the conversation before the altercation happens), fear management, preemptive striking, running, flinch response, and scenario training, as well as the whole gamut of in-fight skills that we need to defend ourselves.

In self-defence, I break the training down into three areas.

PRE-FIGHT

Pre-fight is what happens before the actual physical confrontation takes place. From a self-defence context, everything you do is surrounded by awareness, and all the old cliches are true. The number one rule here is don't be there in the first place. If you walk down a dark alley alone, you are more likely to get attacked than if you are taking a well-lit, busy street.

We must examine our routines and ask ourselves "Where would I attack me?". It's a strange concept, but it gets you to scrutinise when and where in your day-to-day life you are vulnerable.

If we are to defend ourselves, we must first be aware that we are being attacked. Awareness is all.

Our next challenge is confrontation management. We must learn to deal with our fear and adrenaline while attempting to understand the attacker's psychology.

This is one of the key differences between sport and self-defence. In self-defence, the participating parties have different goals, whereas, in combat sports, both people have the same goal.

Criminal attackers generally have three goals.
1. **Take something from you.**
2. **Do something to you.**
3. **Move you somewhere.**

As a defender, you have three goals as well.
1. **Extend and escape.**
2. **Terminate the danger to be able to escape**
3. **Control and restraint. ***

*This is valid only in extenuating circumstances or
if you are a security guard/ police officer.

Unlike a sport, you are not trying to 'win' in the conventional sense. Winning in self-defence is when you are safely behind a locked door.

Now, there will be exceptions to this generalisation, of course. Social violence can be a random encounter with someone who just wants to do you harm. This typically takes the form of the good ol' pub fight where one chap offers the other outside for a bit of a tete-a-tete.

Another exception to the rule is terrorism. Although this is a very scary and serious thing, I have looked at the statistical numbers of it, and you are much more likely to be killed in a car crash or by having a heart attack. Cheery! I'm not saying don't think about it or plan for it, but you also don't need to spend your life living with fear and paranoia.

The next step in self-defence is to assess whether we can give them what they need safely or if we need to fight. This is a vast topic, and a self-defence school will spend a lot of time on it. How can we give them what they want safely, or how can

I make them think I will capitulate so that when I do fight, the attacker is surprised emotionally and physically?

Another big difference between sports fighting and self-defence is the front we put up before the fight. In sport fighting, we always want to look confident and strong. It also helps to look tough and mean! While we may want to do this in self-defence, sometimes it will help us to look meek and mild. By portraying someone who doesn't want trouble and who can't fight, we will have obtained the physical and psychological element of surprise.

Theoretically, if we are viewed as weak and passive, our attacker's adrenaline level will be lower, and their body will be more relaxed. That means if we do have to strike, we will cause the most damage possible.

Using a good surprise shot will also activate a secondary adrenaline dump in our opponent, often causing them to rethink their decisions!

The interview is a massive part of the pre-fight in self-defence and could constitute a whole book in itself. The 'interview' is when the attacker is interviewing you for the role of victim. Much like a job interview, they are sizing you up to see if you will be a good fit. If you are an easy target, you will get the job. If you are a hard target (another great Van Damme movie you should add to your list), they may toddle off and interview someone else. The tricky thing about the interview is that you rarely know it's happening unless you have seen it before.

When I was a green, 18-year-old doorman, I had an experience that helped me to figure this out very quickly. I was on a break at the front of the club, minding my own business, enjoying a well-earned cup of tea from the burger van over the road. I was interrupted in my tea drinking by a drunk man who had recently been ejected from the venue. He spent what seemed like forever slurring his case for re-entry when, out of nowhere, my colleague ran over from his position on the door and hit this man straight in the face, BANG, down he went. As my colleague was putting the man in the recovery position, I asked him, "Whoa, what just happened?" "He was just about to hit you," came the reply. I had totally missed it. The drunk man had hidden his clenched fist behind him and was creeping closer to me to get a good surprise shot in. Thank goodness for my more experienced partner that night! It's not a mistake I have ever made again.

IN FIGHT

This is similar to combat sports training but has a few critical differences. As a baseline, we must be competent in striking, clinching, grappling, and weapons.

From a self-defence perspective, we must also address the potential differences in size, weight, and skill. Multiple attackers and/or defenders may also be possible.

The environment in which we are defending ourselves may also pose a challenge. Uneven surfaces, hard floors and walls, and a host of potentially damaging debris could be waiting to spoil our day.

Another consideration is the element of surprise. In sport fighting, we know when the fight will start; we touch gloves, and off we go. This is not always the case in a self-defence scenario. We need to train to get into the fight from bad positions because we may have been surprised, knocked down, or not had a chance to get into our "fighting stance" before we were actually in the fight.

In addition to the actual fight, we must train how to escape.

This may be a much better option than slugging it out, especially if you are smaller and weaker than your attacker.

Can you open a lock with a key under intense adrenaline? Can you open a car door and lock it quickly from the inside? Can you recognise escape routes or populated spaces while in a frightening situation? Can you run safely? These actions and many more are the kinds of things that we need to add to our training if we want to become proficient at self-defence.

POST-FIGHT

The encounter doesn't just end when the physical fight is over. We have to consider what happens next. Do you know first aid for yourself or others? Are you prepared for potential retribution or legal proceedings? We must also be aware of how this experience will affect us psychologically. Encounters like this can change our lives, so we have to prepare and plan to be able to justify our actions to ourselves afterwards.

Self-defence involves many considerations that go beyond punching and kicking. If this is your primary goal, make sure you find a school that will help you with all of these additional elements.

THINGS THAT A SELF-DEFENCE SCHOOL WILL FOCUS ON:

- **Awareness**
- **Psychology of confrontation**
- **Fear and adrenaline management**
- **Pre-emptive striking**
- **Flinch response**

7. FUNCTIONALITY

Now that we have defined the three areas of martial arts training, we need to determine their functionality in relation to our goal.

I ramble on at my students about my dislike of the word "functional". I explain that without some context, the term functional is being used to shame and put down people who don't conform to its undefined use.

"This martial art is not functional, and if you are training it, you are wrong."

"This strength training is functional, and if you aren't doing it this way, you are doing it wrong."

My question is functional for what? Is a hammer better than a screwdriver? I don't know, it depends on what you are going to use it for. Oh, on a little side note, have you ever seen a martial artist put together flat-pack furniture? My goodness, I've never seen palm strikes, knees, kicks, sticks and training knives used in such "functional" ways before!

A particular family may want to participate in martial arts because it helps them overcome a hard time and brings them closer together. Is that not functional? Maybe someone is struggling with addiction and needs something physical to focus on to help them on the road to recovery. This is functional, too, in its own way.

Each school will also define their "function" depending on its valued objectives. Some schools put a lot of stock into having great fighters and will organise their training around producing the best competitors they can. That doesn't mean you are wrong if you don't want to train like a fighter or step into a ring.

Conversely, if you are at a school that teaches mainly katas but are dying to get into the ring and have a go, you aren't wrong either; you are just in the wrong place. Hopefully, your school won't tell you there is only one way to do things; they will help you find the place you need to be.

If your goal is to become fitter and healthier and learn a new skill, then maybe a gym that focuses more on art is for you. If you want to be a fighter, then you have to find a gym that focuses on competition. All of these will help your ability to defend yourself, but if your main goal is self-protection, then you need to be at a gym that works primarily on those skills.

Maybe you are interested in learning more about the history of pole axe fighting in 13th-century Germany. If that is your bag, then you do you, but make sure you find some other pole axe-wielding folk to help you on your way!

Remember, not everything has to be objective, but make sure you define your "functionality". As long as the functionality is clearly defined and you are honest about your goals and methods, you should stay on the right track. Being awesome at martial arts is first about aligning our goals with our methods.

I have included a little exercise on the next page to help you determine whether you are on the right track. Write down why you train. Next, write down the goals you want to achieve in martial arts. Across from the goal, write what method you will use to achieve that goal. I have included three examples to get you started. Remember, you can have multiple goals, but the method used to achieve them must be specific to each.

WHY DO I TRAIN?

	Purpose	Goal	Method
1	Fun and relaxation	Move more fluidly	Wooden dummy training
2	Competition	Get fighting fit	Thai pads and sparring
3	Knowledge	Learn about pole axe fighting	Study 13th century manuscripts
4			
5			
6			
7			
8			
9			
10			

8. TRAINING TO WIN

If we train in martial arts for an objective purpose, we are ultimately trying to win. That can be in the ring, cage, mat, or for self-defence. Whatever it may be, we must be better than our opponent in one of these things:

FOUR WAYS TO WIN

1. **Skill**. We will win if we can perform our techniques better than our opponent under pressure.
2. **Attributes.** If we have better attributes than our opponents, we will win.
3. **Tactics.** We will win if we can successfully use our tactics and deny the opponent theirs.
4. **Luck.** Sometimes, we just get luckier than our opponent. (I really try not to rely on this one!)

From a sporting perspective, if we can be better in the first three areas, then the only way that the opponent can beat us is with luck. To be competitive, you have to have at least one or two of the top three in your favour. For instance, if you are an exceptionally fit MMA fighter, it may not matter if your opponent is more skilled than you if you can wear them down and make them so tired that they can't use their skill.

One of the most challenging things to come to terms with in self-defence training is that you may not match your opponent in terms of skill or attributes. In most self-defence cases, you will have to rely on your tactics to be able to win as the attacker has probably selected you because they think they can win in the first two areas.

I've also noticed that the better we are at the first three, the better our luck seems to be. As Thomas Jefferson said, *I'm a great believer in luck, and I find the harder I work the more of it I have.*

TOOLS, TACTICS, AND ATTRIBUTES

At my school, I organise our training into three areas: Tools, Tactics, and Attributes. These areas relate to and overlap each other, so when you improve one area, you will improve them all.

Tools

This is where we hone the actual techniques that we are going to use. Am I rotating fully into my punch? Is my guarding hand in the right place? Am I bringing the punch back quickly and to the right place? These are all the little details you will constantly work on throughout your martial arts training. There will always be room for improvement, no matter how small. I always tell my students that the better you become, the more zoomed in the microscope gets.

I can't tell you the number of times that I have been backstage in the warm-up area of a fight show and seen people getting ready who have amazing technique on the pads. Unfortunately, as soon as they enter the ring, it all goes to pot because they don't have...

...Tactics

This is your technique's who, what, where, when, and why. Even if you have the best kick in the world, it doesn't matter if you don't know when to use it. Knowing against whom to use what technique and under what circumstances that technique will work is of the utmost importance. Unfortunately, the only way to learn this is to put in the rounds and build your experience.

Attributes

These are all the things that will make your tools and tactics work better. Speed, power, timing, spatial relationship, decision-making skills, explosiveness, dexterity, and flexibility are examples of attributes we need to be able to fight. But nothing is more important than fitness, endurance, and heart. A lack of these three will kill technique and tactics faster than anything.

We need all three. It doesn't matter how good your kick looks if you don't have the attributes and tactics to score with it. Also, it doesn't matter how good your tactics are if you don't have the tools and attributes to execute them. Lastly, it doesn't matter how honed your attributes are if you don't have the technique or the tactics to use your body as a weapon. Train all three, and you will have a truly terrifying trifecta!

Tools

**Your
Complete
Game**

Tactics

Attributes

THREE TYPES OF FIGHTER

This will be a sweeping generalisation, but hopefully, it will help you identify who you are fighting. At my school, we divide people into three types of fighters. There are many ways to deal with each type, but I will give you some ideas here. Eventually, I want you to discover your own way of dealing with each.

The Bull

This is the person who rushes you all the time. They provide unrelenting pressure and can be very intimidating for the uninitiated. Usually, I try not to run from a bull. Moving away from someone rushing you is very normal. Your primal brain is telling you to move away from danger! Unfortunately, in this instance, it puts you right in their optimal firing distance and allows them the space to hit you more.

This is the time to stand our ground or move offline. Jam the bull up or make them change direction. Like the matador, draw them in, step to the side, and counter, but for god's sake, don't run away, or you will likely get the horns! We will talk more about pressure in chapter 17.

The Runner

This is the person you just can't get hold of. You charge after them, and they float away, picking you off as you blunder your way forward.

To be honest, these people are really annoying to fight against! These guys want you to rush in. Don't fall for it, don't chase them! Usually, I recommend standing and waiting for a runner to come to you so you can counter them. Alternatively, you can move away from them. See if you can draw them closer to you before you pounce. If you can get a runner's weight on the front foot, that's your moment to move forward. If running is not your thing, you can methodically and safely move forward and try to corner them before you pick them apart.

This is like a butterfly fighting a bee, both floating and stinging. On that note, what's wrong with a jellyfish? It floats and stings. Also, it's like water!

Float, sting, be like water, I can do it all!

The Counter-Fighter

For me, this is the trickiest person to fight. They stand their ground and always have an answer for everything you do. It's frustrating, for sure. Against these folks, you are now going to have to be sneaky. Feinting and faking are the order of the day. Connive to survive. I just made that up. You don't have to use it.

This nicely leads us to our next principle, which is similar to the idea of three types of fighters but on a more technical level.

DON'T BOX A BOXER

This is a Bruce Lee adage. He said don't box a boxer, don't kick a kicker, and don't grapple a grappler.

If you are fighting a boxer, you are better off kicking or grappling with them. If you are fighting a kicker, you should be boxing or wrestling, and of course, if you are faced with a good grappler, your objective is to kick or box.

You can take this to mean whatever technical strategy you like. Of course, if you are in a boxing match, it's not a good idea to kick them! But if your opponent is good on the outside, you need to be inside working the body.

This reminds me of Kevin Rosier's interview after his first match in the very first UFC. The interviewer asked him what his strategy was going in. His response was, "Let him hit me!" Now, that is a very tough strategy to use in a bare-knuckle event!

Unfortunately, he lost his next fight when Gerard Gordeau repeatedly stomped on his head and body. So, I guess you could say, if your opponent's strategy is stomping, don't lie down!

It makes me scratch my head when I hear fighters say in their pre-fight interviews that they are going to stand and trade punches with a noted boxer or try to out-wrestle a champion grappler. Unless you are markedly better in an area than your opponent, do something else. Remember, don't always do what is good for you; do what is worst for your opponent.

OCCAM'S RAZOR

Occam's Razor is a superb principle that says the simplest solution is usually the best.

Remember the story of Alexander the Great and the Gordian knot? The knot was so complex that it was said that whoever untied it would become ruler of the known world. Alexander, in his wisdom, just slashed through the knot with his sword. Essentially, that's Occam's razor - or sword in this case!

Especially in competition, the simplest strategies and techniques often win the fight. Many fighters have successful careers with a strong jab, cross, and devastating low kick.

Look at Ronda Rousey. She is a well-rounded martial artist but won most of her fights with an arm bar. Even better than that, her opponents knew the armbar was coming and still couldn't stop it from happening.

We often feel like we should be using things beyond the basics, or maybe it's better to do the fancy stuff. I see many new people who have clearly spent a lot of time watching high-level fighters on TV. They come to sparring and have difficulty staying balanced to land a jab but are still trying to throw spin kicks! It's great fun to watch, but it's probably not the most effective learning method. Remember, your favourite fighter on TV started with the basics, too!

As the old acronym goes, K.I.S.S.! (Keep It Short and Simple)

NOTES ON TRAINING TO WIN:

- **You can win in one of four ways: Skill, Attributes, Tactics and Luck. Being better in two out of the first three is preferable.**

- **Make sure you are training in Tools, Tactics and Attributes to be your best.**

- **Think about who you are fighting and what tactics work best against them.**

- **K.I.S.S. = Keep it short and simple!**

9. THE CUBE

I ramble on and on about the cube to my students. They tell me that if I ever end up in a padded cell (it could happen), I would cover the walls with drawings of the cube.

The cube is the optimum body, hand, foot, and head position to fully utilise the rules of the particular activity that you are participating in. Every sport has a different cube, or "ready position".

Yes, yes, I know. My wife also tells me it's a cuboid, not a cube! Cube, cuboid, or phone booth, you can decide what works for you!

You find football (soccer) players have a different ready position to rugby players. Footballers tend to run more upright to be able to leap over sliding tackles at a moment's notice. On the other hand, rugby players tend to run in a more braced position as they are getting ready for the crunching hits from the opposing team. The cube for Football and Rugby is very different.

Let us compare Boxing and Muay Thai to illustrate the differences in the cube depending on the sport's rules.

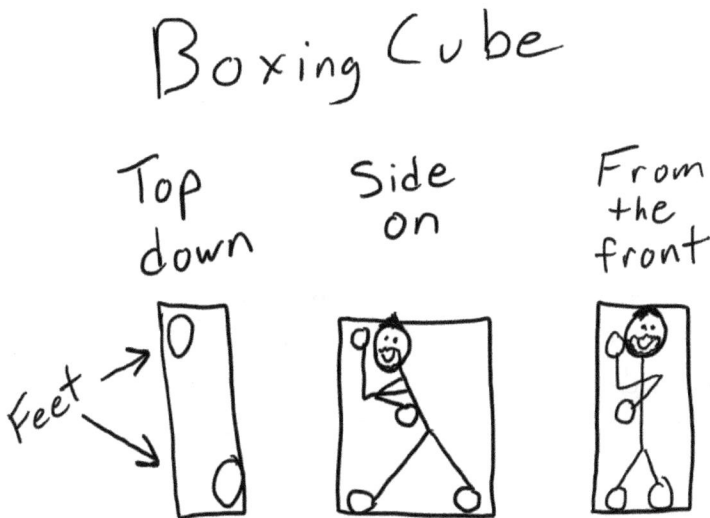

You can see from the elegant drawing above that boxing has a short and narrow cube. In boxing, we want to be more hunched over and side on to present a smaller target to our opponent, that gives us a low and thin cube. Muay Thai on the other hand has to deal with low kicks, knees, and clinch so tends to have a wider, taller cube.

Muay Thai Cube

I break the cube into three parts: Posture, structure and base.

POSTURE

The position of your head and spine

In boxing, your head may be slightly lower, and you may be turned side-on to limit the target area of your body. You may also keep your head constantly moving to present a moving target to your opponent.

While this is an excellent posture for a punching-only art, it would leave you vulnerable in an art that includes kneeing and kicking.

If you practise Muay Thai, your posture should be more upright, with your head relatively static and your body a little more square. This will allow you to block low kicks, and deal with the pressure of knees, and clinch.

Muay Thai people tend to keep their heads in place and

evade when necessary to maintain good posture. If they broke their posture to keep their heads moving, as a boxer might do, they would corrupt their base and be vulnerable to low kicks.

Every action we take with our posture structure or base affects the other two parts of the cube. We must be careful about each movement to prevent the cube from breaking.

Posture also applies to your techniques. When you throw a punch, what does your posture look like?

If you throw a cross but don't step in with your lead foot, you may end up leaning forward. This changes the direction of the force you generate and sends your power down towards the ground. It can also leave you out of balance and in a vulnerable position.

Different arts perform their techniques differently depending on the rules of their sport. Here are two types of round kicks: one from Muay Thai and the other from Tae Kwon Do.

Now, both of these kicks are right, and both are wrong. The only difference is the why. The Tae Kwon Do practitioner needs to lean back to get as much reach and flexibility as possible to land those high kicks while being close to the opponent. This is great for that particular rule set.

On the other hand, the Muay Thai person scores on effect, so they have to maintain their posture and maximise force coupling to make that kick as hard as possible. You are also allowed to catch kicks in Muay Thai, so you need to maintain an upright posture to be able to fight back when your leg is trapped.

When you are next in training, have a look at your posture. What does it look like in your stance and during your techniques? Is your posture where you need it to be to be able to do what you want to do?

STRUCTURE

The position of your hands and arms

For the majority of martial arts, the general consensus is to keep your hands up and protect your head. That makes sense because it's where your brain lives! But how far up should I have my hands? How much brain should I protect?

In boxing, if you are not that bothered about your looks, you can get away with just covering your chin, which is one of the body's off buttons! Boxers also keep their elbows tucked in tight to protect their ribs from punishing body shots.

In Muay Thai, however, a different structure is needed. With head kicks and elbows, we need to have our hands higher. Having the hands closer to the temple will stop elbows from cutting our eyebrows and hopefully cover punishing shins to the head and neck. Having the guard slightly out from the head in Muay Thai also helps us defend against the opponent clinching our neck directly. Remember the number one rule in Muay Thai... don't get kneed in the face! Your mother will never forgive you.

The same applies across martial arts and changes depending on the range or circumstance. If someone was on top of me in the mount position in a grappling competition, I may keep my elbows in and hands protecting my neck and each other, but in an MMA event, I better keep them high so I can defend against any strikes that rain down.

In stick fighting, my weapon hand may move consistently when I am in long-range to present a moving target to my opponent. As soon as the distance closes, I must alter my structure to a solid position in order to block effectively.

It is also important to keep an eye on your empty hand in single-weapon fighting. When I am at long range, I tuck it behind me to prevent it from becoming a target. Once we reach blocking range, I place it on my chest so it is poised to spring into action with trapping or striking.

Next time you train, look at your hands and ask why they are there. Are they in the optimum position for the rules you are fighting under? We need to figure out the why before we address the how, what, where, and when. Muhammad Ali often dropped his hands in a fight, but he knew exactly why and possessed the attributes to pull it off!

BASE

The position of your feet and legs

As we all know, footwork is the most essential part of any sport, except maybe darts.

My brother-in-law is a tennis coach, and he has sadistically spent hours running me side to side on the court with a massive basket of balls, trying to improve my ground strokes.

"Just step like this," he says while I'm scrabbling to keep my feet underneath me. Split step, step across, hit the ball from low to high, all while the ball is flying at you at 70mph.

Ahhhh, so much to remember! But funnily enough, when I started to understand why my feet needed to be there, it made the shot much easier.

After a cognitive phase of (literally) walking myself through the correct steps, I started to take care of my foot position subconsciously, and my game improved.

The same exact thing happens in martial arts. What are the game's rules, and where must my feet be for the optimum application of movement, attack, and defence? Here are three examples of bases from three different styles of combat sports.

In boxing, we stand side-on to our opponent to present a smaller target area. You aren't allowed to strike the legs or back in boxing, which makes this tactic very successful. To this end, we must have our feet closer on a vertical plane. Our lead toe is almost on the same vertical line as our rear heel. Our lead foot will be pointing at the opponent's lead foot. This position allows us to throw good heavy shots with power and gives us the linear base to deal with pressure.

Boxing Base

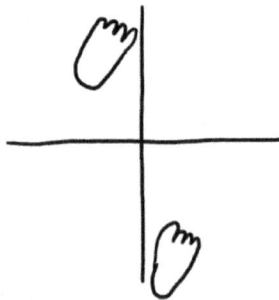

Let's look at a different set of rules. In any sport where we can kick to the leg and block with the leg, we will have to have a slightly more diagonal stance.

If I used the boxing stance from the previous page, my leg block would have to go up and then across to defend successfully, which is one motion too many to get there in time.

Kickboxing and MMA necessitate more movement than Muay Thai, so we must maintain a longer base. MMA fighters, in particular, need to retain the ability to move forward and backward to escape or sprawl when an opponent shoots in for a takedown.

Kickboxing/MMA
Base

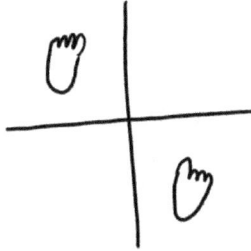

Muay Thai tends to have a shorter but wider stance than boxing or kickboxing. This has a lot to do with range. Gambling plays a big part in Thai boxing; the betting folk and the crowds don't want to see fighters running away. To this end, Muay Thai fighters tend to be just in kicking distance as their default position. Meanwhile, kickboxers, boxers, and MMA competitors usually have a default position outside of kicking distance. Because of this default starting position, there is less bouncy, evasive footwork and more stable preparation for blocking.

The rules also necessitate the ability to deal with punches, kicks, knees and elbows anywhere (almost), as well as clinch and kick catching.

Muay Thai Base

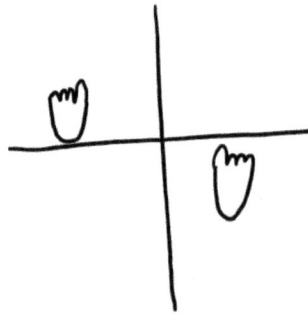

The cube consists of posture, structure, and base. If one breaks, the others can topple. So, in the beginning, we must consciously ensure we keep them all in the right place. Eventually, with practice and experience, we will maintain them subconsciously and move on to breaking our opponent's cube.

Breaking the opponent's cube
You have the gist of this cube idea now, right? So now we need to flip it and break our opponent's cube.

Just as we need to protect the three parts of our cube, we also want to capitalise on the opponent's flaws in their posture, structure or base. Do you have techniques that score most of the time? These high-percentage techniques usually do something that breaks one or more parts of the opponent's cube. As the adage goes, the best time to hit someone is when they can't block it.

A lovely example of this is the cross, lead hook, and rear low kick combination. The cross gets the opponent to cover up and become rigid. It also starts to make them put their weight forward to the front of the cube to resist the pressure.

Next, the hook uses that forward pressure and guides it to the side, putting all the opponent's weight onto their lead leg. Now, you can land the low kick without them being able to block it! Sneaky, right?!

Using the five ways of attack that you will learn in chapter 11, will help you pick apart your opponent's cube and make them crumple like a cheap suit!

NOTES ON THE CUBE:

- **Posture = head and spine.**

- **Structure = hands and arms.**

- **Base = feet and legs.**

- **Find the optimum cube for your game.**

- **Protect your cube when static, attacking and defending.**

- **Break your opponent's cube.**

10. TECHNIQUES: GOOD, BAD OR INDIFFERENT

"That technique is crap!" "Wow, that technique you used was amazing!" I hear statements like these every day in my gym. There is an endless debate about which techniques are better than others, which you should practise and which you should throw onto the rubbish pile of "bad" martial arts moves.

To me, this is an interesting discussion because the poor ol' techniques have no say in the matter!

Are techniques good or bad, or are they totally indifferent? I look at techniques as tools. They are inanimate objects, just ready and waiting for us to use them. Generally, when we comment on a technique, we are commenting on a particular person's performance of that technique or perhaps our own ability not to perform said technique.

Imagine if you were watching a friend put up some shelves. As they hammered in a nail, they smashed themselves in the thumb. Would you say that the hammer was rubbish? Or perhaps the performance of the hammering technique needed work? (Maybe you would say, "Why the heck are you putting up shelves with nails?")

50

Same thing in martial arts. It's the performance of the technique that counts. As my coach, Ron Balicki, says, "It's not the technique's fault if my lame ass can't do it".

Some techniques can be more complex than others. They may require a person to have better timing, attributes, and fight IQ. Some techniques are applicable in fewer places than others, so they are less available. Some require the stylist to have higher physical attributes. A jump-spinning 720 tornado kick is usable for fewer people than a round kick to the leg, but that doesn't make it a "bad" technique per se.

We can divide techniques into High, Mid, and Low percentages depending on their complexity, range of availability, and attributes needed to perform them.

Can you remember the showtime kick? That's where you jump off the side of the MMA cage and then kick the opponent in the head. When that first happened, the world was staring open-mouthed at their TV sets because right up until that moment, the showtime kick was "bulls@$t". It didn't even have a name. Then, the right guy came along with the right attributes, the right fighting IQ and made it happen.

This reminds me of a story my coach Ron tells. He works on films as a stuntman and fight choreographer. He said that on one shoot, a young up-and-coming stuntman came down to the set, and the guys asked him what he could do. He said he had been working on a trick he had seen in another movie. He proceeded to show the guys the move. The guys stared agape at the young lad. Finally, they said, "Don't you know that in that movie they did that move with wires!"

The young stuntman didn't know it was done with wires, so he hadn't put the limitations of that in his mind. He just went ahead and did it.

In 1967 everyone was laughing at Dick Fosbury and his weird

new high-jumping technique. In 1968, he won the Olympic gold medal with his weird Fosbury flop, and nobody was laughing any more (except, I assume, Mr Fosbury). The Fosbury flop is now the universal technique for High Jumpers.

The moral of these stories is that we shouldn't limit ourselves before trying something just because we have heard it doesn't work. It doesn't matter whether it works for anyone else; what matters is whether it can work for you.

Another trap we want to avoid is saying this art or that style is good or bad. Instead, I always advise my students to say, this particular art isn't right for me at this time. I genuinely believe every style or system has something to offer if you look hard enough.

Dan Inosanto is one of the greatest martial arts researchers of all time. He is a martial arts scholar, practitioner, and genuine boss-level master. He is a perpetual student and never stops looking and learning.

One of my favourite stories about Dan was when he met a young boy at a seminar or class somewhere and asked the boy what martial arts he was training. The boy told him and proceeded to teach Dan some techniques from the art. Happily, Dan let the boy have his moment and congratulated him on doing so well. Of course, Dan didn't mention he'd created the art the boy proudly demonstrated. That's some serious humility! What a superstar!

When my coach Ron was a young man coming up in the ranks with Dan Inosanto, he was once taken to another school to watch the instructor teach. Dan sat serenely as my coach writhed with frustration. He thought, "Man, this is a waste of time. What garbage!"

They left after four hours of watching, and on the way home, Dan asked Ron what he had learned. He said to his mentor, "Nothing. It was garbage. Why did we sit there through all that?" Dan turned to him and said, "Well, some of it may have been, but did you see how he did this? And this is how we could apply that." My coach was stunned and enlightened. Inosanto was looking deeper. He was looking not only at what was but what could be. Ron has since devoted his career to researching any martial arts he can get his hands on.

Sometimes, it takes four hours of watching to learn one new thing. The longer you study martial arts, the harder you will have to look for new ideas, but trust me, they are out there. Beauty is in the eye of the beholder! Or beer holder? I can't remember which.

From a competition perspective, it can be of great help to constantly study new arts to find new ideas that will help improve your game. Just like finding new ways to train your fitness, there are thousands of new ways to update your technical game.

Don't just dip your toe in when you are studying new arts. Dive into the art, study it, and figure out their "why". Try not to be coloured by your own preconceptions. You will gain much more if you approach it with an open mind and an empty cup.

Why do they structure their art that way, what is their goal, and how do they achieve it? This will make it more relatable to your game.

Then, bring the ideas back and implement them into your personal expression. Remember, you can change the technique to suit the game, but never change the game to suit the technique. That leads to the training in a vacuum, and unless you are training for art, it's never helpful.

I immensely enjoy adapting techniques to different games. Although the technique may look completely different from its original form, the concept may still work in different environments. I have a theory that you could probably make any technique work in a pressured environment if you had the right training methodology and adapted it to suit your needs.

Have a look at different arts, but see beyond how it looks in its original form. How would it look from your perspective? Where could it fit if it looked slightly different than it does?

I know, I know. You will say, "But Matt, doesn't that change the art? It's not the same art anymore if you adapt it." And I will then say, "I know, I know, but does it matter as long as it suits your goals?" It only matters if it matters to you.

Then you will say, "Wow, that's deep."

Then I will say, "Yeah, I know, right!"

A good few years back, one of my students was fighting in MMA and was doing really well. He later went on to become a UK champion, but for one of his earlier matches, I showed him some arm bars from the Filipino martial art of Kali. Not usually known for its grappling, right? In his next bout, my fighter used this unusual armbar we had worked on. It was brilliant because as the announcer called the fight, he paused and tried to figure out what the submission was. "Armbar" was the verdict!

What's interesting about this is that the opponent had never seen the technique before and wasn't sure how to get out of it. Surprising the opponent with something they are unfamiliar with is a great way to win. Sun Tsu said the height of strategy is to attack your opponent's strategy. Forming a strategy about something you haven't seen before is hard!

Techniques are also eternal. Another good reason not to dismiss techniques off-hand is that they may become useful later in your progression. There are techniques I learned 20 years ago that I put into the storage attic of my mind only to dust them off when I was able and ready to use them. I may not have been ready for them when I first learned them, but after years of training, my attributes and fight IQ were better, and those old techniques that were "useless" before were now relevant.

Another excellent reason for researching other styles, methods and techniques is from a coaching perspective. Even if a technique or method doesn't work for you as a martial artist, hang on to it as a coach because it may be a good fit for one of your students.

I keep a rolodex of techniques in my head (or at least on my computer!) so when I see a student who seems like the right fit for one of them, I can pass it on to them.

NOTES ON TECHNIQUES:

- **Techniques are inanimate objects that require someone to perform them to be good or bad.**

- **There are high, mid, and low percentage techniques.**

- **The technique is not at fault if you can't do it, you are!**

- **Keep researching. Your next high-percentage technique is out there.**

- **Keep hold of that knowledge regardless of whether it is good for you at the time. You or your students may need it later.**

11. FIVE WAYS OF ATTACK

Bruce Lee studied a lot of fencing – amazing, I know, right?! His brother Peter was a champion fencer at his school and taught Bruce much of what he learned.

Bruce Lee's Jeet Kune Do uses many fencing terms of attack, including riposte, counter-riposte, reprise, remise, disengage, cutover, redouble, beat, bind, envelopment, arrest, feint, invitation, absence of touch, change of engagement, preparation of attack, attack on preparation, direct attack, indirect attack, and compound attack.

Bruce then organised all of these and more into five general categories. They are:

1. **Single direct attack (SDA) or single angulated attack (SAA)**
2. **Attack by combination (ABC)**
3. **Hand or limb immobilisation attack (HIA)**
4. **Progressive indirect attack (PIA)**
5. **Attack by drawing (ABD)**

I use the same five ways of attack, I just define them slightly differently so they cover a broader spectrum of arts. Let's look at each and how they can be useful to you.

SINGLE DIRECT ATTACK (SDA)

A single direct attack is as obvious as it sounds. One punch, one kick, one knee, one headbutt, one butterfly eyebrow, or one spinning flying dragon claw – it's all a single direct attack.

These are the least sophisticated attacks, but as we know, simple is effective!

For a single direct attack to land, we must have good attributes. Because our attack has to travel so much further than our opponent's defence, we need our initiation speed, timing, spatial relationship, power, and non-telegraphic motion to be tip-top.

Surprise is a key element in a single direct attack. If we can genuinely surprise the opponent with our SDA, we stand a much greater chance of landing the attack.

From a self-defence perspective, we can legally launch a pre-emptive strike at the attacker when we genuinely feel we are in physical danger (UK law 2024).

In this situation, we can lower the opponent's adrenaline level by claiming passivity and making them overconfident of their victory. This will lower our opponent's psychological and physical defences. This means that when we throw our surprise SDA, it will have a greater chance of doing a high level of damage.

In a sporting scenario, we can use our SDA in a number of ways. Testing an opponent's defence, setting up another attack, keeping them at bay and trying to knock them out are just a few ways we can effectively use our SDA.

ATTACK BY COMBINATION (ABC)

Muhammad Ali and Prince Naseem Hamed, amongst others, are masters of combinations. Hamed regularly landed flurries of ten or 12 strikes unanswered against a bewildered opponent.

Combinations are a great tool to overwhelm our opponent's ability to react cognitively to our attacks. By overwhelming an opponent, we can start to land strikes on places that are not protected and cause significant damage. The combinations themselves can cause damage or may be used to set something else up entirely.

From a stick-fighting perspective, I may rush the opponent with a series of X strikes to entice them to block my stick, thereby making their stick static. This will allow me to pick an unprotected target for my stick, punch or kick.

Combinations can be applied in three ways: defensive combination, committed combination, or a blitz.

Defensive combination

A defensive combination is a barricade of strikes you throw as your opponent tries to apply pressure. You can do this while standing your ground, fading back or stepping to the side.

Committed combination

A committed combination is an attack in which you step in to land your shots and then back out without (hopefully) being hit in return. In Savate, they call this touching without being touched. This is an excellent strategy against someone you don't want to be close to.

Blitz

The blitz is a powerful tool from a sport and self-defence perspective, and is fantastic for overwhelming people. Many people have a hard time dealing with an unrelenting barrage of pressure and are literally hard-pressed to come up with a solution.

This can also be very useful in overcoming technique log jams. I coached a Muay Thai fighter who was very talented but struggled to get going in the early rounds of one of his fights. He was showing the opponent too much respect, not committing to his strikes, and began to take hits. He lost the first two rounds with this mentality. In the corner before the third, I told him to use only the boxer's blitz.

A boxer's blitz is essentially running at the opponent with alternating straight punches.

He went straight out in the next round and blitzed the opponent. Immediately, the game changed because he didn't have to think about anything, and the opponent was having difficulty dealing with the pressure. He went on to win the fight after he got his composure back. So sometimes clearing the mind and focusing on just running the opponent over can have a significant effect.

In self-defence, this can also be very effective for a smaller person defending themselves against someone bigger. Sometimes, single attacks have little effect in this situation due to the size difference. A well-timed blitz may overwhelm the attacker enough to give them enough time to get away.

HAND OR LIMB IMMOBILISATION (HIA)

The momentary immobilisation of a limb to facilitate hitting.

That is how Bruce Lee describes the art of trapping. Essentially, he is saying, how can I clear my opponent's defences out of the way so I can hit them?

Many arts use trapping to achieve this goal. Some are more sophisticated than others, but all serve the same purpose. Boxing and Muay Thai have more clubbing and jamming traps, while Wing Chun, Kali, and Silat, among others, have complex combination traps.

I have an analogy that I use with my students about a tree.

I'm sure you will find it as silly as they do!

I ask the class what they would do if they were driving along a road and came across a fallen tree blocking their way.

Someone will shout,

"Go around it!"

"Yes," I say, "go around that tree."

Someone else will say,

"Go a different way."

"Exactly," says I, "go back and try a different way."

Then the cheeky sod in the class will say,

"Get a chainsaw!"

Ha Ha Ha. But that is precisely how I see trapping: you remove the barrier!

Take that, clever clogs!

Think of trapping as isolation. You either stop them from being able to defend so you can hit them or stop them from being able to hit you so you can hit them.

Like all our other techniques, trapping can be used in three pressures: offensive, defensive, and neutral.

An offensive trap is when you are on the attack before you trap. The trap opens a gap for you to continue your barrage. For example, if you were throwing a boxing combination but your opponent was covering well, you could simultaneously knock one of their guarding hands down and punch them in the face. This would clear a route for you to continue your combination.

An example of a defensive trap is if someone blitzes us, we can use our long guard to jam up their punching ability while we land a low kick to their leg.

Neutral traps don't happen often but can be surprising if done correctly!

Imagine someone intimidating you and pointing a finger right in your face, saying they are going to assault you.

Your hands are up saying, "Please, I don't want any trouble". All of a sudden, you slap their hand down and blast them in the face, WHAM! That moment of surprise will definitely give you time to follow up or get yourself out of there!

There are many kinds of traps. Single traps, compound traps, jamming, and even long-range clinching can be considered trapping. When grappling, we may trap an arm before we lock it to make it harder for our opponent to escape. When we are stick fighting, we can grab our opponent's stick, momentarily stopping them from hitting us while we hit them.

I break trapping down into reference points. These are points of connection that give us a moment of familiarity from which we know what to do.

Have you ever been lost while walking or driving? Do you remember that glorious feeling of relief when you finally recognise something you know? It's a relief because you know how to get home from that spot you recognised, right?!

Well, a reference point is just that - somewhere you know how to get home from. Of course, "home" in this context means punching your opponent in the face!

When we use one arm to trap one of their arms, we have eight potential reference points. I have drawn it for you in a very clear and understandable way. (Sarcasm)

These are top-down drawings, with you on the bottom and your opponent above. And yes, those are arms, you cheeky so and so.

1. **Your left arm is outside of their left arm**
2. **Your left arm is inside of their left arm**
3. **Your left arm is inside of their right arm**
4. **Your left arm is outside of their right arm**
5. **Your right arm is outside of their left arm**
6. **Your right arm is inside of their left arm**
7. **Your right arm is inside of their right arm**
8. **Your right arm is outside of their right arm**

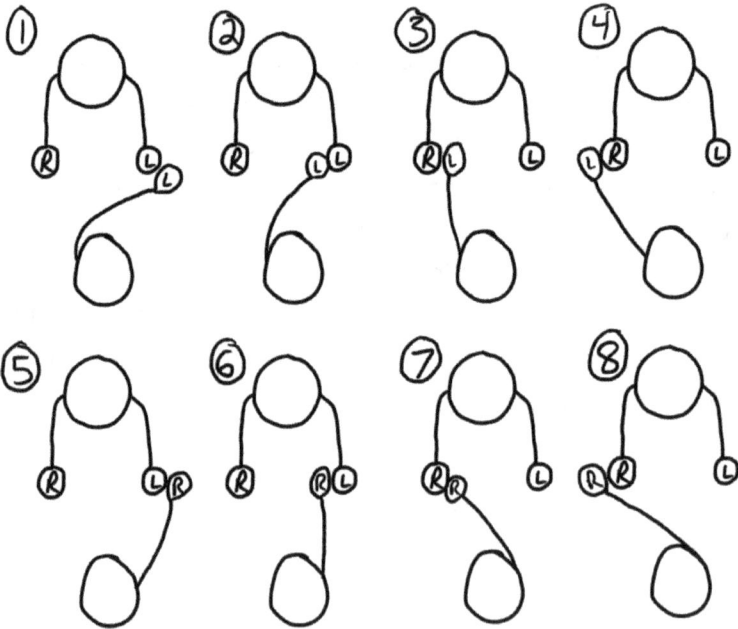

When both of our arms are involved with both of their arms, we have four possible reference points.

1. **Both of our arms are on the outside of both of their arms**
2. **Both of our arms are on the inside of both of their arms**
3. **Our left arm is outside their right arm, and our right arm is inside their left arm.**
4. **Our left arm is inside their right arm, and our right arm is outside their left arm.**

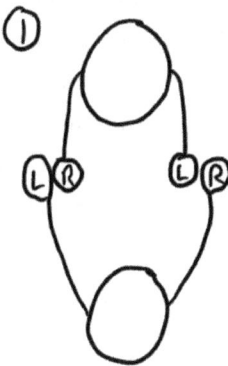

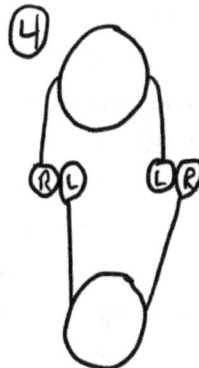

From any of these reference points, we can slap, pull, push, scoop, jerk or snag their arm(s) out of the way and land a good shot.

Trapping can be complex and frustrating to learn, but it's definitely worth researching because once you get the hang of it, it will add a new dimension to your game that is hard for your opponents to deal with!

PROGRESSIVE INDIRECT ATTACK (PIA)

It does what it says on the tin, right? It progresses indirectly to the target. All progressive indirect attacks start with what I call a negative attack and transition into a positive attack.

A negative attack is not meant to damage but to bait the opponent into making a mistake that we can capitalise on. Positive attacks are the big guns we use to do damage. Essentially a negative attack doesn't hit, and a positive one does.

There are many definitions of PIA out there. Eventually, you will have your own way of describing them that makes sense to you. Here's how I categorise them.

Change of line

This is the truest form of progressive indirect attack. A strike that progresses indirectly to the target. Now, in theory, it does this without retracting first.

If I throw a jab towards the opponent's face and they attempt to parry it, I can, at the last moment, run the jab around the guard and turn it into a long hook. In Wing Chun and JKD, they call this jau sau or running hand. This particular strike takes on the trajectory of a helix, so it doesn't actually retract as it corkscrews its way to the opponent's face.

If you have ever seen boxer Roy Jones Junior, you know that he uses this incredibly effectively with his fake hook-to-uppercut attack.

The question mark kick is similar to this. The starting point is a front kick or low round kick that, at the last moment, turns into a high round kick.

The same idea can be used in a grappling environment. Imagine you are in the top half guard position. Swinging your leg over your opponent's head could make them think you are trying for a near-side armbar. When they pull their arm away to defend the armbar, we keep the motion going and smoothly transition to a far-side knee bar.

In Filipino martial arts, this is sometimes called enganio. Enganio means to deceive or to trick. If you had a weapon, you could start the attack with a forehand strike to the head and, at the last moment, as their block comes up, change it to a low backhand strike to the leg using the same sweeping motion.

Generally, you can use PIA from inside to outside, outside to inside, high to low, and low to high. It's a fantastic tool for keeping the opponent guessing where you will strike next!

Feint

To me, feinting is throwing about 90% of the technique before changing it to something else. The feint doesn't necessarily have to be the same progressive movement as it did with the change of line. For example, imagine that you throw two positive jabs at your opponent's face, then on the third attack, you feint the jab and throw a positive cross to the body.

There is a delicate balance to be found here. The more I commit to the feint, the more the opponent will believe it, but also, the more likely they are to be able to defend it. So I need to sell it just enough to get a reaction, but not so much as they can stop it.

Fake

I define faking as using the arm, head, body, or leg motion that precedes an attack to deceive the opponent. This motion may be less than 10 per cent of the actual strike. So, it is not a strike as such but the part people read before the strike happens.

If I use the example from above, I would throw two positive jabs, dip my shoulder on the third one as if I were about to initiate another jab, and then throw the positive cross to the body.

The most important factor when throwing any of these PIA techniques is that the opponent must already believe the attack will hurt them if they don't defend it. That way, the opponent will try to defend when you throw your set-up, allowing you to bypass it.

When faking and feinting, you have to be Houdini! You have to make them believe! You need to sell these techniques to the opponent so they will buy them. We could wander off into some weird analogy about a market and haggling, but I'm going to sidestep that one and just say we need to convince our opponent with our legs, arms, body, head and face that we are going to hit them.

When you are fighting normally, vary your movements so they are not predictable. But when you are using PIA, make them a little more obvious so your opponent can see it coming and fall into your trap. Be careful, however: if your trap is too obvious, they will spot it and possibly counter you for your trouble.

We can chart this in a lovely little graph. Let's call this the sliding scale of obviousness!

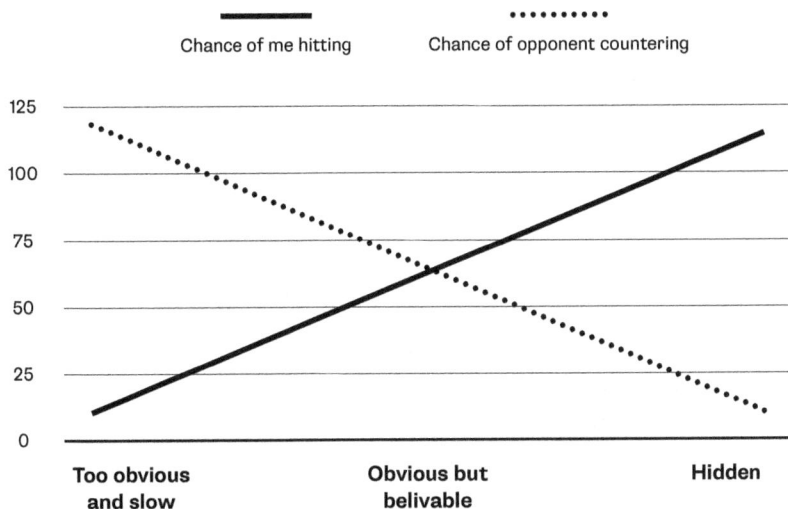

Chance of me hitting .... Chance of opponent countering

ATTACK BY DRAWING (ABD)

First, you need a pen, a piece of paper and then... no, I'm just kidding. That joke always reminds me of the Monty Python sketch about how to disarm a man wielding a banana. First, you eat the banana, thus disarming him! Classic.

Attack by drawing involves lulling an opponent into a pattern and then changing it. This is, more often than not, used in conjunction with PIA or ABC.

I often think of ABD as code-breaking. We look for patterns in each other's code, trying to spot a way to decipher what they will do next. Top-level fighters do this very well. It's almost like they are reading your mind.

Now, here is a sentence for you to get your head around:

I don't want them to see a pattern unless I want them to see a pattern.

I know, paradox much!

Attack by drawing usually happens in one of three ways.

1. **Offensive**
2. **Defensive**
3. **Footwork**

Offensive

An offensive attack by drawing involves repeatedly using the same attack to programme your opponent into a predictable defence you can circumvent.

Often, an offensive attack by drawing is used in conjunction with PIA. If I throw two positive jabs at the opponent's face, then change the pattern with a fake jab and a low cross to the body, this is using ABD and then PIA.

Defensive

I always think of a defensive ABD as a mousetrap. (A humane one, of course!) By offering something of ourselves as the cheese, the opponent, or mouse, in this scenario, is tempted to nibble it. Then, as they attempt to nab the cheese, we close the trap around them.

A classic example is if I drop my lead hand slightly to offer the opponent a free punch to my face. As they attempt to hit me, I intercept them with a kick to the stomach.

From a grappling perspective, we often use the defensive ABD to escape a bad position. If someone was on top of us in mount position, we could pretend to flail around on the bottom "accidentally", offering our straight arm for an arm bar. As they go for the arm bar, we sit up and escape the lock and the bottom position.

Here's the rub: your attributes must equal the draw you make. If I offer my face for the punch and I'm too slow, or if the distance is too close and I get drilled in the mush, that's not a good draw. Make sure your cheese doesn't exceed your grasp!

Footwork

Footwork is the final way to use attack by drawing. We could also categorise this as movement, but more often than not, it's going to be with our feet.

Using a draw with footwork can be a fantastic way to deal with a fighter who is a constant runner. Sometimes, you can't get a hold of these people, and to continue to chase them may get you in trouble.

It's time to use a footwork draw! Take a small step backwards away from your opponent, enticing them to step forward. You may do that a few times in a row to show them it is safe to come forward. Then, just as they step forward for that last time and put their weight on their lead leg, BANG, you hammer them with a low kick and take some air out of their tyres.

One tip to remember when using ABD is to hide your draw. If the trap is obvious, they will safely spring your trap and counter it with one of their own. It can become a real battle of the minds: who is drawing who?

I'm always on the lookout for my opponent's trap because if you can do it to them, they will, of course, try to do it to you. Set your traps, but remember to vary your strikes, defences, and movements so you don't fall into theirs. Keep scanning their faces and bodies for clues that they are setting a sneaky piece of cheese for you!

Of course, all five of these attacking methods can be combined to make you a super fighter! After you have mastered each of them, put them together. Here's a sequence to give you an idea:

1. Fake the jab (ABD)
2. Fake the jab (ABD)
3. Fake the jab (ABD)
4. Low inside kick (PIA and SDA)
5. Slap their lead hand down and hit (HIA)
6. Cross, hook, cross (ABC)

Combining the five ways of attack together in different ways will really boost your ability to be successful against an opponent with a good defence, so give it a go!

NOTES ON THE FIVE WAYS OF ATTACK:

- **SDA = Single direct attack.**

- **ABC = Attack by combination.**

- **HIA = Hand immobilisation attack.**

- **PIA = Progressive indirect attack.**

- **ABD = Attack by drawing.**

- **Mix them all to keep your opponent confused as to what is coming next.**

12. FIVE WAYS OF DEFENCE

Just as there are five ways of attacking, most defences can be divided into five categories. Some techniques fall into one of the five categories, while others display traits from multiple categories.

DEFENSIVE DEFENCE

This is the turtle. In the turtle, our limbs come towards our head and body to defend. This defensive idea is usually most beneficial when we are surprised, under overwhelming pressure, or need to close the distance quickly. Essentially, whenever we don't have time or space to react to individual attacks, we are better off just turtling up!

This is also a bit tricky because we are working against biology here. When a stimulus is introduced too quickly, we humans flinch. Normally, that flinch means putting our arms out and pushing away danger. Sometimes, however, pushing our arms out to defend against danger is not the best option when we are facing someone who is running at us and smashing their hands into our faces.

There is also the very typical issue of turning away. Most beginners who come to our gym do this at the start. When punches fly, they turn their heads away and try to escape the attacks. Very sensible if you are turning and running from a sabre tooth tiger, but when it comes to a boxing match, it may be a hindrance!

So, instead, we have to try to fight our biology, keep our heads forward, arms in, and focus on protecting our vital spots.

Covering is the primary tool in this category. Any time we bring our hand to our head or body, it is a cover. Crazy Monkey is a fine example of a defensive defence and an excellent get-out-of-jail card.

You can perform the crazy monkey defence by putting your hands on your head, tucking your chin down, lifting your shoulders, and moving your arms alternately up and down.

Initially, the goal is to constantly change the gaps in your defence so that it is hard for your opponent to find a hole. As you get better, you will start to be able to time your arm movements in correspondence with your opponent's strikes. Crazy Monkey is a fantastic defence, but remember, it's only short-term. You need to do something else to get out of danger quickly, or your opponent will eventually find an opening!

OFFENSIVE DEFENCE

As the name implies, offensive defence is more proactive than defensive defence. This category includes catching, parrying, limb destruction, long guard, and active covering.

Anything that extends to the edge of your cube could be considered an offensive defence.

These defences are much more commonly used when the pressure is lower, and the distance between you and your opponent is greater. When we have more time and space, we can defend with a higher level of cognition. Here are some options when it comes to offensive defence.

Parrying

Parrying is essentially about moving a straight attack off its intended trajectory. To do this, extend your hand to the edge of your cube and swat the incoming attack into a new trajectory that goes past your face instead of into it!

The same idea is used for scoop, slide, and elbow deflect.

Long guard

The long guard is an active defence that Muay Thai fighters use to great effect. This structure puts one or two of your limbs on the direct line of attack while simultaneously covering your head and chin. The cool thing about the long guard is that it creates a physical and psychological barrier that the opponent has to go around. So, in theory, you have forced them off the most direct line of attack.

The same applies to the long guard as it does to the crazy monkey; it won't protect you forever! For it to have done its job, you will need to move into the clinch, move out of distance, or follow up with some counters of your own.

Limb destructions

A quick note on limb destructions: Please, please, please don't do these in sparring! Even in a sports fight, you come across an interesting moral question. Are you prepared to win at all costs, even if it means permanently disabling your opponent? I know I'm not. Self-defence is another story. If you are being attacked, I want you to destroy everything that comes your way!

Everyone saw Chris Weidman as he spiked Anderson Silva's leg in half. As Anderson crumpled to the ground, we all knew it was the end of an era. We didn't know then that Chris Weidman had trained to do that on purpose. Unfortunately, the wheel of karma kept rolling, and the exact same thing happened to Weidman in a later fight.

These two injuries were debilitating and career-changing. These sorts of injuries take months and sometimes years to physically heal, never mind the lasting mental damage. So, it's worth asking the question: Do I want to be responsible for the downfall of another sportsperson? I would always tell my fighters to avoid intentionally imposing this kind of lasting damage. Just because it isn't against the rules doesn't mean it won't leave a mark on your conscience.

I love the attitude in Thailand. It's very different from the win-at-all-cost attitude that sometimes pervades the Western fight world. These Thai fighters are there to do a job and earn money for their family. They also respect that their opponent is there to do the same thing. They have some of the deadliest legal techniques at their disposal, but they choose not to use them. They often show the technique lightly so the judges can acknowledge it, but it doesn't cripple their opponent. When you fight every week to feed your family, this is a symbiotic way to operate.

Anyway... limb destruction means trying to destroy the attacking limb. We could use our knee to spike an oncoming kick or our elbow to destroy an oncoming punch. In Kali, we call this defanging the snake. If we are stick fighting and someone tries to hit us with a weapon, one of our best defences is to step out of the way and smash the hand of the opponent. Hopefully, this will make them drop the weapon, thus defanging the snake. Even if it doesn't damage the hand, it will certainly plant a psychological seed in the opponent's mind: "every time I try and hit them I get hurt!". These work, by the way. I once had a student break his hand through a boxing glove while doing this, so please be careful when you train your limb destructions!

ESCAPE AND EVADE

I'm going to lump escape and evade into the same category as they are very similar. (It also gives me five ways of defence, which ties in nicely with the five ways of attack. I'm all for symmetry!)

To me, escaping means avoiding the attack but putting myself out of range to counterattack. Evading is the opposite; I avoid the attack but remain in a good place to launch a counterstrike.

Most of the techniques in this category can be done both as an escape or an evasion. These include but are not limited to slip, duck, bob and weave, sway back, leg evasion, and, of course, sucking the belly in!

SIMULTANEOUS ATTACK AND DEFENCE

This is my personal favourite defence! I love the idea that every time the opponent tries to hit you, they get hit. That is so demoralising! It also puts a real mental barrier in the mind of your opponent.

It's a bit like Pavlov's dogs! Every time the opponent hits you, you smack them on the nose and say, "No! Bad dog!" (Don't actually say that in sparring, okay!)

Simultaneous attack and defence could be a block and hit or an evasion and hit. The critical point here is that the defence and attack happen at the same time.

If your opponent threw a jab at you, you could simultaneously parry and punch them in the face. Alternatively, when they threw the jab, you could slip your head to the outside of their arm and at the same time jab them in the body.

This also works for kicks. If the bad guy goes for a round kick to my body, I can catch their leg and kick their supporting leg out simultaneously. I can also forgo the catch and just step to the side and cut-kick their supporting leg away.

Cut you down to Size!

I suppose it goes without saying that simultaneous attack and defence is one of the trickiest counters to time correctly. Normally, you are behind the game when defending, so save this counter for when you see the attack coming early, and you have enough time and space to pull it off.

Another way to accomplish this is to force them to use the technique you want to counter with ABD.

In the past, students have asked me how I could counter them so easily. I wish I could say that I have gained a mind-reading ability after all these years of training! But no, I ruined the magic trick when I told them I left them no other option but to attack with the technique I wanted to counter. "Ah," they always reply, "but that's so simple."

"I know," I always reply. "Simple is as simple does."

INTERCEPTION

This is the defence that Bruce Lee rated above all others. In fact, he rated it so highly that he named his art after it. Jeet Kune Do, of course, means way of the intercepting fist or foot, or in my house, fork!

Interception is by far the most challenging defence to pull off. You need a little bit of mind-reading to get this right! I say mind-reading, but actually, the ability to read body language and pre-contact cues is what is essential here. How early do you see the attack coming? If you are experienced at reading your opponent, you will see their attack before it launches and stop them with an attack of your own.

I saw a great example of this concept in a documentary hosted by Dr Robert Winston.

The programme showed how birds perceive things earlier than humans do. That is why birds, flies, and other flitty little things are so hard to catch. They seem to see things almost in slow motion, or what would look like slow motion to us.

Great fighters like Saenchai and Floyd Mayweather are the same. They see attacks way earlier and can counter them much faster. That's why the top fighters are usually good at interceptions.

Early perception, lightning reflexes, and pinpoint timing all contribute to intercepting someone's attack. One way to help with that early perception is to learn to recognise pre-contact cues. In poker, these are called tells. They let us know what someone is going to do before they do it.

Does your opponent pull their hand back before they punch? Do they blink before they kick? Do they step a certain way before they shoot a double leg? These are all tells that will give you a slight advantage when intercepting.

When you first start training, you don't see the punch until just before it hits you on the nose. That's okay; it's normal! It will get easier after you have had a few thousand punches thrown at you. You will start to see that attack coming much earlier, giving you more time to deal with it.

Now, here is a super secret training tip to enhance that. When holding pads for your partner, don't waste that time thinking about what's for dinner! Use it to look at what your partner does before they throw their attacks. That way, you can pick up some experience at seeing attacks coming in and not waste a second of training time! You're welcome!

Now that you have a general idea of the five ways of defence, start categorising your techniques. Where do they fit along the pressure spectrum? When is the perfect moment to use which defence?

Remember, just like in attack, our defence can become predictable. Be aware of how you are defending and change it up. That way, your opponent will never figure you out!

NOTES ON THE FIVE WAYS OF DEFENCE:

- **DD = Defensive defence.**

- **OD = Offensive defence.**

- **EE = Escape and evade.**

- **SAD = Simultaneous attack and defence.**

- **INT = Interception.**

- **Mix all five so the opponent won't find a gap in your defence.**

- **Be careful with destructions, please!**

13. CENTRE LINE AND CONE OF BALANCE

CENTRE LINE

The centre-line principle is used mainly by Wing Chun and JKD practitioners, but I have yet to see an art that doesn't contain something similar. I use two types of centre lines in my teaching. They are:

Self-centre line

Imagine you stuck a pencil in the centre of your chest. Wherever you turn, this pencil is your self-centre line. The images below are a top-down view of the self-centre line. I'm sure you can tell from these exceptional drawings how the centre line moves as you do.

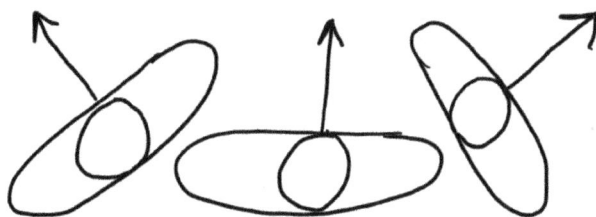

Mother Line

The second centre line we use is called the mother line. If you can imagine that you and your opponent both had a pencil sticking out of the top of your heads and there was a piece of string connecting the two, this is the mother line. Again, use this incredibly clear top-down drawing to see how the mother line connects you and your opponent even as you move.

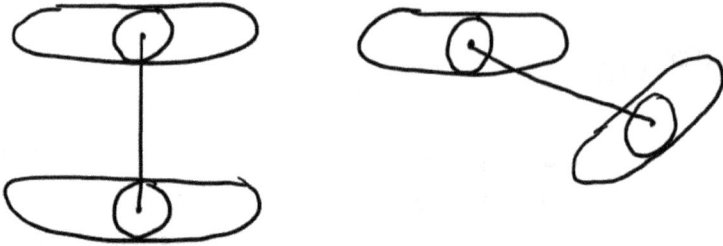

Now, this becomes important because in a perfect world, we want our self-centre line on the mother line but the opponent's self-centre line pointing somewhere else.

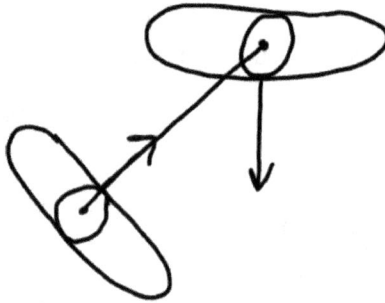

If we can accomplish this, it means all of our weapons are facing the opponent, and theirs are facing away from us. Most martial arts use this idea in some way or another. Any time you hear the phrase "move offline", that is what you are attempting to do. If you are able to move offline, it means the opponent has to readjust to be able to attack or defend. This means you are one beat in time ahead of them, which is a great moment to land an attack.

CONE OF BALANCE

The cone of balance is a concept we use to determine where we need to manoeuvre the opponent to cause them to lose their balance. (It's a clever name, right?)

The size of the opponent's base will determine how far we have to push their hips or head to disrupt their balance.

If the opponent's base is small, we only have to move the hips or head a relatively small amount to make them topple over.

If the base is large, we have to move the hips or head far further for them to be off-balanced.

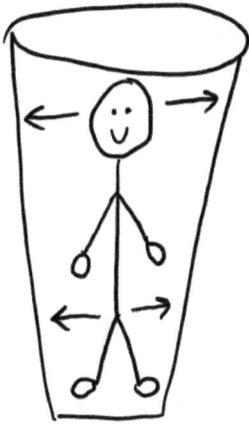

Small
Base

Large
Base

Of course, this principle only works if the base is fixed and static. If you push your opponent's head backwards, they can adjust their base and maintain their balance. But if you stand on their feet as you push their head backwards, they can't adapt their base, and down they will go!

You can isolate your opponent's base by sweeping or tripping, by putting a foot, knee, or hand in the way of their stepping, or even by making them take a big enough step so they become grounded.

Now, because most people don't stand with their feet together in a fight, they will present both a narrow and a wide base at the same time. If you look at their foot position like a square (or a cube, if you will!), the wide base will be between the feet, but the narrow base will be between the empty spaces, which will be the best place to attempt to use our off-balancing. I know that sounds confusing, so let me use a few of my crystal-clear drawings to help you get the idea!

If someone were standing square on, and you could manipulate them on line A or line B. Which is more likely to put the opponent off balance? It's line A, right?! Line A has only the length of the foot for balance, so it presents quite a narrow cone. (I know those don't really look like feet, and I know one is bigger than the other. I'm sorry, okay?)

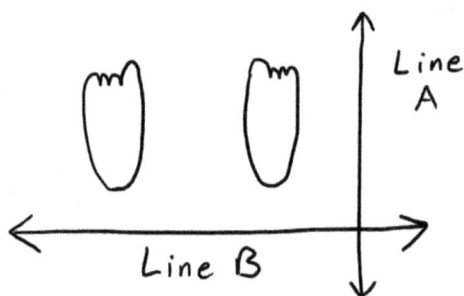

Line B presents a wider cone because the base consists of the space between the feet.

Now, if we adjust that drawing slightly and put the opponent in the left lead, we can see how they always present us with one wide base and one narrow base.

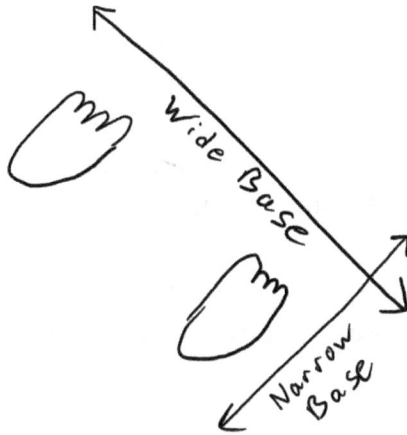

On the flip side, we must also remember to take care of our base. A narrow stance makes you more mobile but less stable. Conversely, a wider stance makes you more stable but less mobile. We need to be able to do both depending on our range and what the opponent is trying to do to us. The farther we are from the opponent, the narrower and more mobile we can be. As we get closer to the opponent, we must widen our base to deal with or apply pressure.

NOTES ON THE CENTRE LINE AND THE CONE OF BALANCE:

- **Self-centre line is a pencil in your chest.**

- **Mother line is a pencil in both of your heads and a piece of string connecting them.**

- **Try to have your self-centre line on the mother line and the opponent's self-centre line pointing somewhere else.**

- The wider the opponent's base, the more you have to move their head or hips to make them fall over.

- Isolate their base so they can't adjust it when you're off-balancing them.

- A narrow base is mobile, but not stable. A wide base is stable but not mobile. Protect your base!

14. A TRIANGLE AND A SANDWICH

In the previous chapters, we looked at the "why" and "what" of your training; now, let's look at the "how".

This description of research and methodology is taken from research-methodology.net

> Research can be defined as "an activity that involves finding out, in a more or less systematic way, things you did not know" (Walliman and Walliman, 2011, p.7).
>
> "Methodology is the philosophical framework within which the research is conducted or the foundation upon which the research is based" (Brown, 2006).
>
> O'Leary (2004, p.85) describes methodology as the framework which is associated with a particular set of paradigmatic assumptions that we will use to conduct our research. Allan and Randy (2005) insist that when conducting a research, methodology should meet the following two criteria:
>
> Firstly, the methodology should be the most appropriate to achieve objectives of the research.
>
> Secondly, it should be made possible to replicate the methodology used in other researches of the same nature.

So first of all, we need to define our training goals.

Our goals will ultimately define our training methods. Whether we train for self-defence, sport, or art, it is essential to consider the parameters and constraints we are working with and to tailor our training accordingly.

For instance, if I wanted to maximise my self-defence training and had only two hours a week, I probably wouldn't spend that time doing rounds of Muay Thai on the pads. While this would benefit me in the long run, it wouldn't be an effective training approach given my time constraints if my goal were to improve my self-defence skills. Instead, I would be more inclined to focus on the interview, pre-emptive striking, flinch response, awareness training, running and scenario training.

The same would apply if my goal were to be an MMA fighter. My time would not be best spent learning Wing Chun wooden dummy forms or knife defence. Of course, these may be sound long-term supplemental training, but they do not directly help me achieve those goals.

Once we have established the goal and our method, we need to structure our training time to obtain optimal results.

The I triangle and the cognition sandwich go hand in hand to help you develop the goals in your training. Let's have a look at them now.

THE I TRIANGLE

The "I" triangle is the main training methodology we use at our gym. Matt Thornton of Straight Blast Gym created this method, which my coach, Karl Tanswell, taught me. The I triangle comprises three parts.

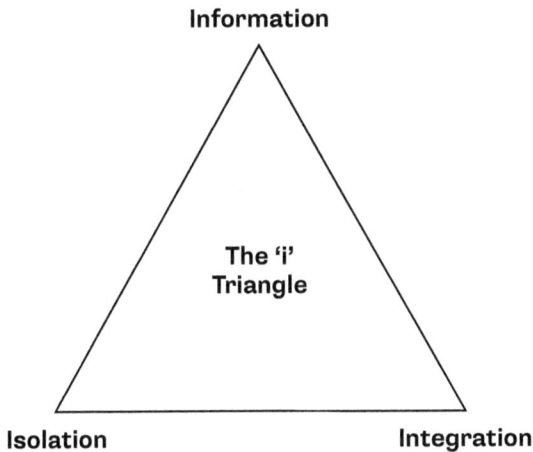

Information

The 'i'
Triangle

Isolation   **Integration**

Information

This is the raw material - the technical learning of a jab, a kick, an arm bar, footwork, defence, or strategy. We usually learn this in a vacuum to get the basics of how the technique works without resistance.

For example, imagine you are learning how to throw a hook punch. You might stand in front of the heavy bag and practise your hook, focusing on the technical and mechanical parts of the movement without any pressure or decision-making distractions.

Information training can be done with a partner, on pads, on any striking target, or even in thin air. I really like to incorporate the information stage of the training into the warm-ups in my classes. That way, the students are ahead of the game when it comes to the next stage of the class.

Remember, while it is fun and important to perfect your techniques with no resistance, you will need to add in the other steps of the I triangle if you want to make your techniques useful!

Isolation

Isolation is the stage of the training where we subject the technique or strategy to an increasing spectrum of pressure and constraints. The isolation phase requires us to develop a delivery system. A delivery system is any method that contains:

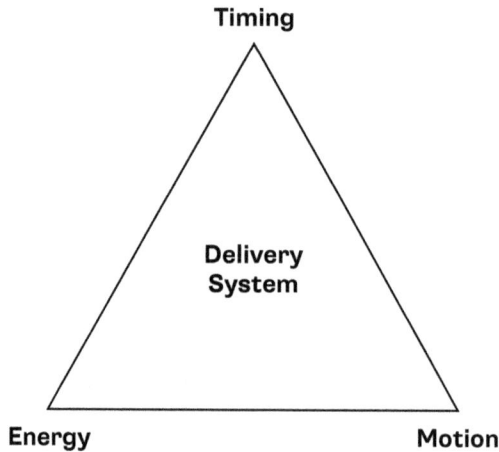

```
            Timing

           /\
          /  \
         /    \
        /      \
       /  Delivery \
      /   System   \
     /              \
    /                \
   /_____\
  Energy            Motion
```

A delivery system can be almost anything we want, as long as it contains those three items. This keeps the training "alive" and gives us real-time feedback about the success or failure of our technique.

Isolation training helps us bridge the gap between learning a technique and sparring. It allows us to create a graduated series of drills to help us acclimatise to the pressure of the final goal.

Depending on your level, you may have to start with a basic drill that has very few distractions and build up from there.

I think of it like training to run a marathon. You usually wouldn't get up on your first training day and run 26 miles! You may start with two miles, then build up to five on your next outing.

The same applies here. If you start with full power and pressure, the only thing you will learn is how to get beat up!

Here is an example of how I would build something up in my class:

Let's say the technique we want to work on is a leg shield to block a low kick. Let's assume we have completed the information stage and already have a good technique for our leg shield.

- **Step 1:** I have the student practise the leg block with a partner back and forth to get an idea of how that technique works.

- **Step 2:** Partner A might move around and throw low kicks whenever they like, and partner B has to try to block it.

- **Step 3:** Now, we add a distraction. Partner A can now box and throw the leg kick whenever they want. This teaches partner B to block the low kick while dealing with pressure from the boxing.

- **Step 4:** Partner A can only move and throw the low kick this time. Partner B is boxing in this round and trying to block the kick as it comes in. This teaches partner B how to block while throwing punches and applying pressure.

- **Step 5:** Both partners are boxing. Partner A kicks when they like, and Partner B tries to block the kick. Now, partner B is able to block under a spectrum of pressure.

If you are a coach, this is the moment when "coaching" makes sense. We can adjust our students' technique under pressure so that it makes sense to them why they need to do it differently. Correcting people in the technical phase is very hard, as it lacks context. In a vacuum, they just have to take your word for it, which is a less ingraining way to learn.

Maybe step 6 of this particular plan could be on the pads. We have an open pad feed, where the feeder holds for anything they like and then randomly throws the low kick, which partner B has to try to block.

This methodology allows us to create just about any isolated drill we like. We can focus on any technique or strategy we want to work on, and engineer the drill to help us achieve a particular goal.

If you are at a higher level, you may not need as many steps, but you may need to make the drills more challenging by adding more pressure and distractions.

If you are just starting out, you may need to add even more steps to ensure some degree of success. The cool thing is that you can tailor-make the training just for you!

In these isolation drills, I want you to be successful 60%-70% of the time. This way, you get to know what it feels like to succeed at doing the correct thing without it being too easy. If the success rate is less than that, we must make the drill more manageable to bring the success rate up. If the success rate is too high, we have to amp it up and make them able to do the technique under greater and greater pressure.

I often used this with my fighters. If I identified something in their game that needed work, I would set out a series of isolation drills to help them develop that area.

Here's an analogy for you. (Keep in mind that I know next to nothing about cars.) If you hear something sounding funny in your car's engine, you take that part out and fix it up before replacing it to see if it runs better. Does that help? Probably not; I didn't say it was a good analogy!

Let us move on!

Integration

Integration involves returning the technique to the whole. This is the point at which you return to hitting pads or sparring and assess how well you apply the technique after your isolation training. Regardless of the type of integration training you are doing, I want you to keep the thing you were focusing on at the forefront of your mind, so you continue to practise it and monitor how you are doing with it. A terrific way to do this is through goal-oriented sparring, or GOS.

Have you ever heard the phrase "leave your ego at the door"? I bet you have.

I'm not entirely sure this is possible. Since our ego is partly responsible for keeping us safe, it's hard not to try to win when someone is potentially trying to hurt us.

Goal-orientated sparring helps to focus that "winning" drive on something else. When I spar, I always have a particular goal in mind. It could be something technical like trying to land as many left kicks as possible or maybe only going for triangle chokes when I grapple. It could also be a specific strategy like not stepping backwards or trying to corner the opponent.

Having a specific goal in sparring makes winning about doing what you are trying to do rather than just beating the opponent. It makes it about you. It also ties in with the I triangle so that you are always learning when you are sparring. Give it a go next time you spar!

I tend to break down my classes like this:

- 10% Information or technical training (often in the warm-up)
- 40% isolation training
- 50% integration training (pads or sparring)

If you use a training breakdown to something similar to this, it will definitely help you grow!

You must be working up an appetite with all this reading. Ready for a snack? How about a cognition sandwich?

METACOGNITION

One of the most common things I hear from new students is, "That doesn't feel natural." And I happen to agree - none of this feels natural. We are ultimately learning to override our naturally instinctive movements.

While sometimes the movements we have ingrained from biological programming or previous training can be beneficial, they can often get us in trouble when we are dealing with a new set of rules.

The tricky part is that we must consider our movements before they become trained responses. This can be a long and frustrating process.

To do this, I use a method I call the cognition sandwich. (This is mainly because I love sandwiches!)

The cognition sandwich allows us the time and space to think our actions through and repeat them under increasing levels of stress until they become "natural" to us.

Cognition sandwich

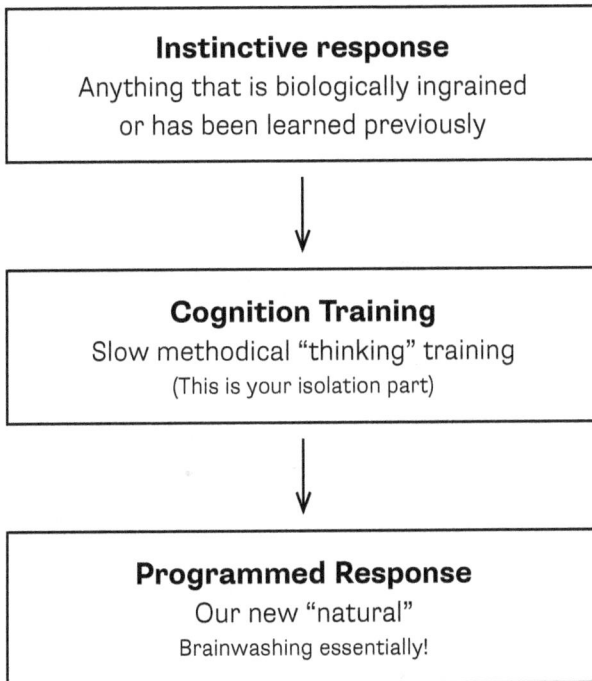

Instinctive response
Anything that is biologically ingrained
or has been learned previously

↓

Cognition Training
Slow methodical "thinking" training
(This is your isolation part)

↓

Programmed Response
Our new "natural"
Brainwashing essentially!

Now, I'm sure this will be controversial, but here it goes. I'm not a big fan of the term muscle memory. Sorry, I know it's catchy, but our muscles don't have memories. I prefer the term neural pathways. All of our cognition training is about setting up new neural pathways.

I am going to drag Dr Robert Winston into this again. I saw another fascinating documentary he presented that explained the creation of neural pathways. (You are getting a sense of what I do in my spare time.) The good doctor stood at the edge of a crevasse with no way across. A professional climber was there to assist Dr Winston in getting to the other side.

The climber threw a rope across the crevasse and fixed a point on the other side. He then shimmied across the first rope with the second rope attached to him, and with the one crossing, he strengthened the connection. Back and forth, the climber went across the chasm, continually strengthening the connection between the two sides. By the show's end, he had made a full rope bridge that Dr Winston could easily walk across.

This is the same for us when learning new things. Like crossing the crevasse, the first connection is the toughest and must be thought out most. After that, it gets easier every time we cross that gap. Eventually, we will have a programmed response or a new neural pathway - or muscle memory, if you must!

This sort of training is definitely tough on the ego. It's hard to take our time and slow things down, especially if we just want to get stuck in! But trust me, it will pay off in the long run.

We have a great saying at our gym:

"Fast and Sh*t...still Sh*t!"

A less vulgar way to say that is from my coach, Paul Pearson: "The slower you train, the faster you learn".

NOTES ON THE I TRIANGLE AND COGNITION SANDWICH:

- **Information = learn the technique under no pressure.**

- **Isolation = create games to practise the technique under different levels of pressure.**

- **Integration = try the technique in the normal game.**

- **Satisfy your ego and learn faster with goal-oriented sparring.**

- **Train slow, learn fast.**

15. RANGE BULLSEYE

This beautiful bullseye is a pictorial definition of the tactics and tools we should use at each particular range or distance.

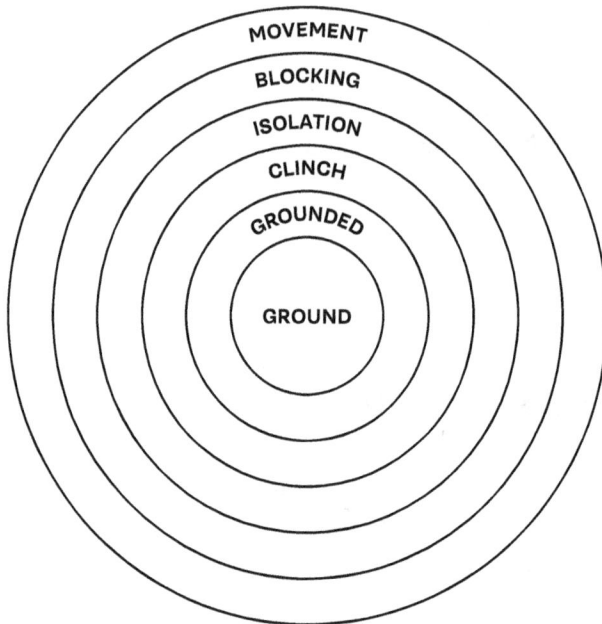

There are many ways to describe the different ranges in combat. They could be defined as long-range, middle-range, and close-range, or we could call them kicking, punching, trapping, and grappling ranges.

Please feel free to describe the ranges in the way that works best for you. I use this particular definition because it helps you to recognise the primary tactic and structure you have to adopt at a specific distance. Before I define these ranges, I just wanted to note that you could end up in one of these ranges in three ways.

1. You just end up there. There's no pressure either way; it's just where you find yourself.
2. You put yourself there. This might be part of your tactics to beat a certain type of fighter.
3. Your opponent puts you there. Maybe they are trying to keep you within a certain range. The sneaky beggars!

Whatever happens, knowing where you are and what to do next is a good thing.

Each sporting rule set and self-defence goal will have slightly different versions of what is optimal in each range. If you fancy it and have some spare time, print out the bullseye and fill it out as it relates to your art.

Here's how we break down the ranges in my school.

Movement range

This is the longest distance. As you may have guessed, the primary tactic here is movement. Footwork is super important at this range. Can you move around or away from your opponent safely and in balance? From a self-defence perspective, this is the range from which we will try to escape from our attacker.

In this range, we use principles and techniques that require more time and space.

Defensively, we can use interceptions when our opponent tries to step in to get us. We can also use evasion and offensive defence at this distance, as we have more time to react to whatever our adversary throws.

Offensively, this is a probing range. It is time to use what we call questioning techniques. These are non-committed strikes that are only designed to ask the question, "What does my opponent do when I do this?" This will give us insight into how the opponent reacts and how we can exploit that reaction.

The next offensive tactic we need in the movement range is entering. To engage, we have to potentially cover a large distance without the opponent intercepting us or having them move out of the way. In the JKD world, they call this bridging the gap. Distraction is the key here. Make them think something is going to happen and then change it. (Who's the sneaky beggar now?) If you can combine this with your probing, you will certainly keep your opponent mentally and physically off balance.

Now, your art may or may not use this, but from a self-defence perspective, this is also the projectile range. If you are going to spit or throw something, you will need time and space to do so. Projectiles are used to damage or distract your opponent so you can enter or escape.

Blocking range

At this point, we are so close that we may struggle to evade our opponent's strikes. This proximity makes blocking and maintaining our cube essential. Naturally, depending on the rules of the game you are playing, the tactics may differ.

In boxing, for example, there still may be an element of head movement and evasion, but typically, this is more predicated on presenting a moving target rather than reactionary evasion. However, in Muay Thai, this becomes primarily a blocking-only range.

I define blocking as either deflecting a linear attack away from its intended path or stopping an angular or circular strike from crossing the centre line.

Muay Thai is a good example because it tends to start in this range. Also, because Muay Thai has so many weapons, it must maintain its cube in blocking range to avoid exposing other targets.

Sometimes, our eyes can be too slow at this distance. At our school, we say that action is always faster than reaction unless the reaction has enough distance to catch up.

Imagine I'm going to have a race with Usain Bolt.

I know I know, he's in trouble, right?

The first race is over 20 metres, but I get a two-second head start. I reckon even I could beat him here.

Now, the second race is over 200 metres. Even if I get a two-second head start, he will leave me in his dust.

Defensively, in this range, we must rely on defensive defence. Remember that when the distance is short and the pressure is high, complex motor skills are out the window, and we have to rely on gross motor skills to get us through.

Offensively, our striking is much more varied, as most of our tools are available, but we must ensure we are protected when we throw them. In blocking distance, fakes and feints become less valuable. Here, we want to hit with power and make all our shots count because, of course, if we are in the distance to hit them, they are in the distance to hit us!

Isolation range

Isolation or trapping range is a momentary distraction to gain an advantage in striking, clinching or takedowns. They can be used offensively, defensively or neutrally to simultaneously block and attack, remove a barrier or jam the opponent up. Can you remember HIA from the Five Ways of Attack chapter? This is where you will find all that stuff!

We can also use our tactile sensitivity at this distance. (No, not that kind of sensitivity!)

As mentioned above, at a close distance, our eyes are sometimes too slow. Fortunately, our sense of touch is faster than our sense of sight, so if we are already in contact with our opponent and they attack us, we can feel the change of pressure and deal with it accordingly. Energy drills like Chi Sao, Hubud, and pummelling are valuable for building tactile sensitivity.

Here is a funky experiment to put this to the test:

Have your partner stand an arm's length away from you and have them jab you in the chest as fast as they can while you try to parry it.

Did you get hit almost every time? Probably, and that's okay.

Now start with the same set-up, but this time, put your

hand on the side of their punching hand before they punch. Try to feel when they go and redirect it with the connected hand. More success? Hopefully so!

Just like Bruce Lee said, "Don't think, feel".

But definitely think as well, okay!

Isolation range can be tricky because it is unsustainable. This means we cannot continue to fight in isolation range if the opponent fights back. We must move into isolation range, gain our advantage, and then pop straight back into movement, blocking, clinching, or ground to capitalise on the advantage we have created.

As the late, great Kenny Rogers said, "You got to know when to isolate them, know when to punch them, know when to clinch away and know when to run."

Something like that, anyway.

Onwards.

Clinch range

Now, we are locked on to our opponent and are momentarily equal. This range will be very dependent on the rules and goals of our art. Are you trying to knee and elbow? Turn or throw? Headbutt, gouge the eyes, and bite?

Whatever your goal is, we are now competing for dominance at a close distance. Because every art has a different goal, you will see different structures in the clinch. Greco-Roman and Olympic freestyle wrestling have a much more bent-over clinching style than boxing or Muay Thai. The wrestlers aren't going to get kneed in the face if they bend over, so that makes sense. As with all other ranges, you must ensure that your cube matches the rules of your game.

Grounded is when one person is on the ground while the other is standing up. This is a very tricky situation to deal with.

Most of the time, if we are the ones on the ground, we will try to get back to our feet. However, depending on the game, we could potentially look to bring our opponent down to the ground with us. When we train grounded, we also break it down into movement, blocking, and clinch ranges.

Movement range in a grounded situation is where we are trying to back away to be able to get up. Here, we can use our probing and interceptions to help us achieve that goal.

When we are in grounded blocking range, we are within reach of their attacks, so we must use our legs to try to block their kicks. We can also use various kicks from our backs to try to demotivate our opponent.

In the grounded clinch range, we can use our entanglements and takedowns to off-balance our opponent or bring them down to our level.

Grappling range

In our final range, both people are on the ground. Grappling is an incredibly broad topic that covers positions, transitions, submissions, pins, escapes, set-ups, striking, and more. Most countries around the world have their own versions of wrestling or grappling.

These styles all focus on a particular goal. It could be striking, submission, pin, getting up or moving your opponent somewhere. Some styles use a combination of goals. Just like the rest of the ranges, the tactics here depend on the game's rules and your goals.

I also wanted to mention that these ranges apply to empty hands and weapons. It doesn't matter what you or your opponent is holding; the ranges stay the same. Check out the next chapter for more info on range tactics!

To become a well-rounded martial artist, you need to have

at least a working knowledge of all of these ranges. That way, wherever you end up, you will always have some idea of what to do. I know it's challenging to train in the ranges you don't like or aren't good at, but keep at it, and you will develop a well-rounded fighting style that is all your own.

To paraphrase my coach, Ron Balicki, from his book The Principles of a Complete Fighter, *"To become a complete fighter, we must always seek out failure".* Pg 12.

NOTES ON THE RANGE BULLSEYE:

- **Defining what range you are in will help you pick the correct tactics.**

- **You may choose to be there or be forced there.**

- **Movement range is outside of your longest weapon.**

- **Blocking range is just inside of your longest weapon.**

- **Isolation range is the momentary distraction to gain an advantage in one of the other ranges.**

- **Clinching range is when you are locked onto each other.**

- **Grounded range is one person on the ground and one standing.**

- **Ground is both people on the ground.**

16. RANGE TACTICS

We have examined the different ranges; now, let's discuss what we should try to do in each range.

I've compiled a chart to show what tactics you should use in each range. These are in no particular order and are a general theme for all styles. I have included a blank chart so you can fill it in with specific range tactics for your art or sport. (I'm sorry; I know you didn't buy this book to have to do homework.)

I have also included a section for the Interview. This will only apply if you are training for self-defence, but I think it is important to include it. In my school, we treat The Interview as a separate range.

Now, you may also be asking, "Matt, I do weapons. Where do they fit? I even do projectile weapons. What range is that?"

This chart works for all styles, including weapons, as you will soon see! As for projectiles, it depends on where you project them from! The type of weapon doesn't matter; it's the range you are working in that counts.

Not sure im in the right range

Uh Oh

RANGE	TACTICS
Movement Range	1. Elusive footwork 2. Escape 3. Evasion 4. Defang 5. Probing and interception
Blocking Range	1. Stable deliberate footwork 2. Strong structure to deal with pressure 3. Power hitting
Isolation Range	1. Stop them hitting you 2. Remove barriers 3. Transition in or out when the isolation breaks
Clinch Range	1. Strike 2. Improve position 3. Off balance 4. Takedown
Grounded	1. Strike 2. Create space with movement in order to get up 3. Close the distance and entangle them to the floor
Ground	1. Strike (dependent on rules) 2. Get up (dependent on rules) 3. Position 4. Transition 5. Submission
Interview	1. Extend and escape 2. Diffuse 3. Pre emotive strike 4. Flinch response

You have now filled in each of these ranges with techniques and tactics as they relate to your art. (If you haven't, there is no skipping ahead! Do it, do it, do it! Or don't, I know you're busy, don't worry you can skip ahead if you like.)

When we isolate a specific range, we train our techniques and reactions. But when we train the change between ranges, we work on our decision-making skills. This is one of the most challenging things to become proficient at in martial arts. This is also why MMA is such a powerful style. MMA people are very good at knowing what range they are in, when that range changes, and what they need to do next.

I call the moment a range changes an event horizon. My student, Professor Barry (who you will meet later in the science chapter), came up with that name one day and it just stuck. You have to admit, the name sounds cool right! Just please don't ask me to explain the science!

The drawing on the next page shows all of the ranges as they progress in distance, starting from the top down. Each of the arrows represents a potential event horizon. We need to train each and every one to recognise when a change of range has occurred.

We need to develop specific drills to help us recognise the change in range at the moment it occurs.

Here's an example

1. Let's start with a delivery system of long-range, low-pressure boxing.
2. At some point during the long-range boxing game, partner A will blitz partner B with a series of straight punches.
3. Partner B will try to recognise the range change and react with a crazy monkey defence, clinch and then knee.

In this blank chart, fill in the details of your style and art:

RANGE	TACTICS
Movement Range	
Blocking Range	
Isolation Range	
Clinch Range	
Grounded	
Ground	
Interview	

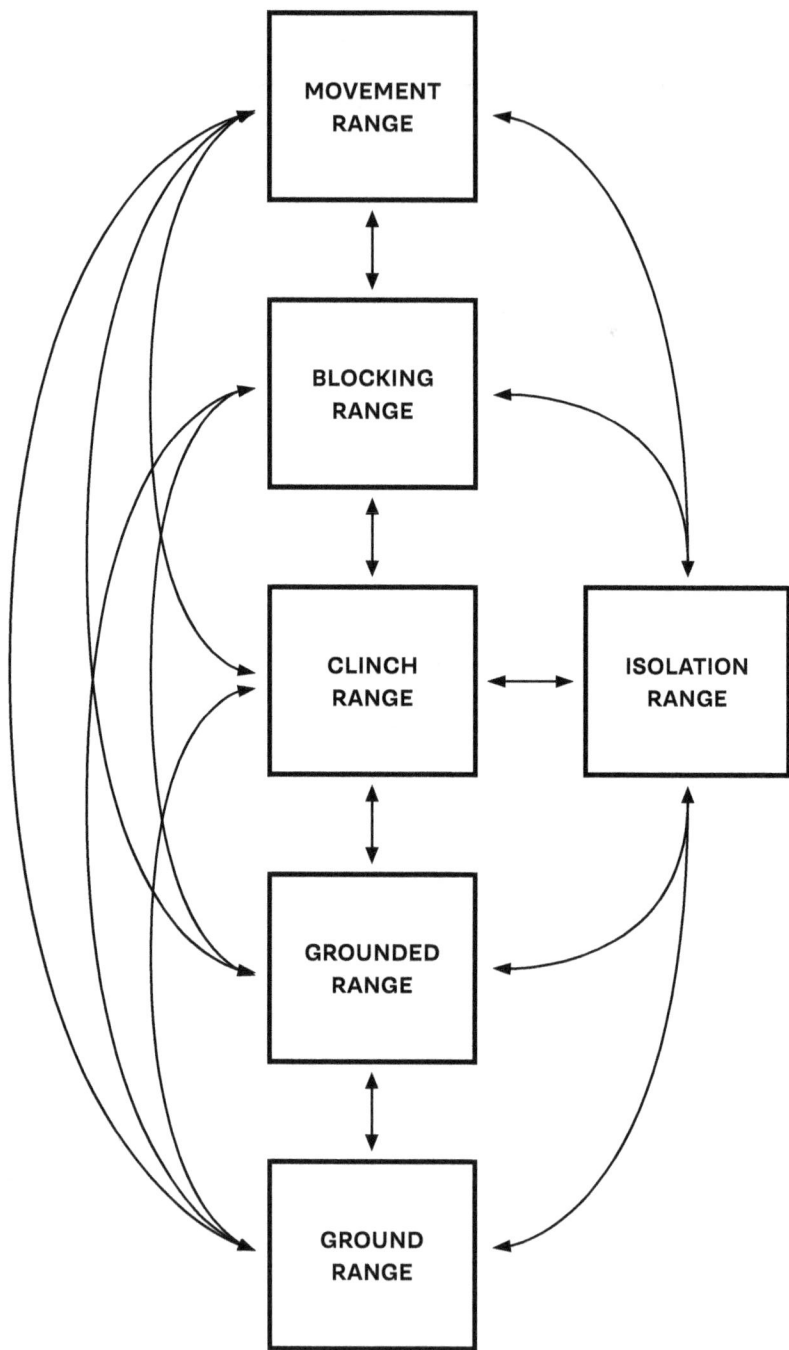

Now, let's add some progressive resistance.

As partner B gets better at recognising and reacting to the blitz, partner A will start to blitz faster, harder, and with less telegraphic motion.

This drill will help partner B recognise the event horizon between the movement, blocking, and clinching ranges.

Okay, you weapon guys and gals, this part is for you! Another benefit of the range tactic chart is that it allows you to evaluate what tactics are available if you are fighting with weapons of uneven length. This will give you an instant assessment of your strategic choices.

For this explanation, I'm going to use these tactics:

- **Evade (move out of the way)**
- **Defang (move out of the way and hit opponent's hand)**
- **Block (can't move out of the way)**
- **Isolate (move in and stop weapon hitting you)**
- **Clinch (lock on)**

If we have weapons of equal size, we can use all of them, right? So what happens if we have weapons of unequal length?

Let's say you have a five-foot-long staff, and I have a two-and-a-half-foot stick. What tactics do we both have?

If you have the staff, you have all of them!

- **Evade**
- **Defang**
- **Block**
- **Isolate**
- **Clinch**

If I have the shorter stick, here's what I have:

- **Evade**
- **Block***
- **Isolate**
- **Clinch**

*Sometimes, I don't even have a blocking range if you are hitting with a lot of power!

What about a knife vs a stick?

Stick person:
- **Evade**
- **Defang**
- **Block**
- **Isolate**
- **Clinch**

Knife person:
- **Evade**

- **Isolate**
- **Clinch**

What about stick vs empty hand?

Stick person:
- **Evade**
- **Defang**
- **Block**
- **Isolate**
- **Clinch**

Empty hand person:
- **Evade**

- **Isolate**
- **Clinch**

Knife vs empty hand?

Knife person:
- **Evade**
- **Defang**
- **Block**
- **Isolate**
- **Clinch**

Empty hand person:
- **Evade**

- **Block**
- **Isolate**
- **Clinch**

Using this approach, you can immediately see what strategy you need to employ against a certain weapon, depending on what you are fighting with.

We can also use this process when it comes to physical or skill-based advantages. If we are fighting someone who is very tall, what should we look to do?

- **Evade**
- **Defang**

- **Isolate**
- **Clinch**

That's right, we need to be all the way out or all the way in!

Or maybe our opponent is really good in the clinch or with takedowns. Now, which parts of the plan are no-gos for us?

Identifying what range you are in, what you can do there, and when it changes will definitely enhance your game, so get playing!

NOTES ON THE RANGE TACTICS:

- **For your specific art, figure out what tactics are good for you in each range.**

- **Learn how to recognise when the range changes so that you can adapt your tactics.**

- **If you know where your opponent is weak, try to be in that range.**

- **When you and your opponent have weapons of different lengths, try to be in the ranges that suit your weapon and avoid the ones that don't.**

17. PRESSURE SPECTRUM

An ice age here, a million years of mountain building there. Geology is the study of pressure and time. That's all it takes really, pressure, and time.

This is the famous quote from Andy Dufresne in the movie Shawshank Redemption. Aside from being an amazing movie, this statement is true for just about everything we do. How much pressure am I under? How much pressure can I deal with? What can I do under pressure? How can I apply pressure?

For our purpose, pressure is inherently related to distance and distance to time. These will be the underlying factors for all of our martial arts training: pressure, distance, and time.

The first thing that most of my first-time fighters said to me the minute they stepped out of the ring or cage was,

"Wow, that guy was really going for me, there was so much pressure".

I would always reply with

"Yep".

That is the game. Unfortunately, the bad guy is also always trying to win.

With that in mind, we have to intelligently introduce pressure into our training. The end goal is that the opponent can do whatever they like with whatever pressure they like, and we can deal with it.

Of course, like running a marathon, we must start small and build up. We must engineer drills that acclimatise us to applying and dealing with increasingly heavy pressure. This is no easy feat, as it is very hard to replicate the violence and maliciousness of a real situation under training conditions. Can you remember the story about the frog in the pot? If you put a frog in a boiling pot of water, it will immediately jump out. If you put a frog in a tepid pot of water and gradually turn the heat up, it won't notice and will eventually become cuisses de grenouille! (Please don't try this at home!) This is exactly how it should feel when we are creating these drills. If done properly, you may not even notice the pressure increasing.

One of the best tools I have found to help deal with educating people about pressure is the pressure spectrum:

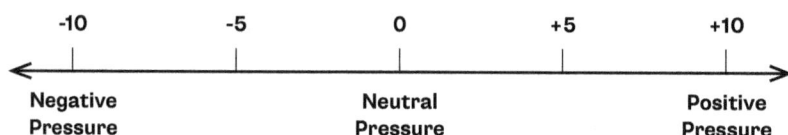

-10	-5	0	+5	+10

Negative Pressure   Neutral Pressure   Positive Pressure

Imagine the diagram above as a football pitch. (That's soccer to all of our North American friends!) Negative pressure is when the ball is in your half, and you are starting to focus on defence and getting the ball out.

Neutral pressure occurs when you show off your fancy footwork near the centre circle while your opponents tentatively try to take the ball off you.

And finally, positive pressure is when you are making a run for their goal.

Do you ever get that sinking feeling when watching your favourite team play? You know, the excruciating minutes when the opposing team circles your goal. They are peppering your keeper with shots, and your defence is desperately trying to get the ball out. They are passing and passing, and shooting and shooting, and you are shouting at the television, "Clear the ball, you stupid overpaid *£%*@!"

Well, you are right to do so because that is, more often than not, when the bad guys score. The same goes for fighting.

The more time you spend in positive pressure, the more likely you will land effective strikes.

Of course, there are exceptions to the rule. Some people are excellent counter-fighters or very good at fighting while going backwards, but for the most part, the fighters that apply pressure correctly win.

A good quote I've heard is: "Applying pressure overrides their ability to defend cognitively."

I don't know who said it, but basically, it means that if I apply enough pressure, my opponent's brain will bypass any conscious thought process and defend instinctively, which tends to be less effective.

Now, obviously, we can't just steam in with all guns blazing; we have to apply pressure in an appropriate and strategic way so we don't leave ourselves open to counterattack.

DEALING WITH PRESSURE

If we are under neutral pressure, we can take the initiative and apply our pressure directly. The problem occurs when the opponent pressures us first. In that case, we must neutralise their pressure before applying some of our own. As I see it, there are really only six things you can do when someone is applying pressure towards you. You can go into it, away from it, to the left of it, to the right of it, over it, under it, or stand your ground and counter it. If there are more you can think of, add them to this list!

Let's have a look at a few of the ideas I use to neutralise negative pressure.

Away from it

Going away from pressure is the most natural thing in the world to do. It's what your brain is screaming at you to do. It's what we have evolved for millions of years to do.

Unfortunately, in this instance it may put us in a worse place to fight from. Remember, the opponent can always run faster forwards than you can backwards. This means that by going backwards constantly, you might be keeping yourself in their striking range. By moving backwards constantly, you are breaking your cube, putting yourself off balance and making it harder for you to block incoming attacks. Also, if you go backwards for any length of time, you are in danger of running out of space. Being cornered is a tough place to fight from! As I said above, there are always exceptions to the rule. If you can fight effectively off the back foot, then go for it! You can draw the opponent in and pick them off, but remember that if you do go away from pressure, try not to do it all the time. Change it up so your opponent doesn't figure out your pattern.

Into it

Sometimes, when the opponent attacks us, the simplest way out is to cover up, step straight in, and jam them up.

To do this, you can use our get-out-of-jail defence, which I call crazy monkey. Here's how to do crazy monkey:

1. Put your hands on your hairline. If you wear boxing gloves, your inside knuckles should touch your forehead, and if not, your palms should touch your forehead.
2. Tuck your chin down.
3. Lift your shoulders.
4. Make all the gaps as small as possible.
5. Slide your right hand up your head so your elbow is in front

of your nose.

6. Bring your right hand back to your hairline, and slide your left hand back this time.

7. Alternate left and right. Repeat as needed.

The aim of the crazy monkey is to alter the openings in your guard, which makes it hard for your opponent to pinpoint an effective strike. Crazy Monkey will protect you long enough for you to close the distance and stop your opponent from hitting you.

It's important to maintain good posture while using Crazy Monkey so you can see what is going on and avoid opening yourself up to other attacks.

What happens after your Crazy Monkey depends on the game you are playing. In boxing, you might just be looking to smother the opponent's attack so you can work their body at close range. In Muay Thai, now you can lock on and start drilling your opponent with your knees. If you are an MMA fighter, this might be an excellent time for some heavy-duty throws. From a self-defence perspective, this is the moment to bring out the big guns of eye gouges, headbutts, knees, elbows and biting.

Moving left or right

Moving offline is one of the most common ways to deal with pressure, and while it may be common, it certainly isn't easy! Essentially, this is you being a matador. If you get the bull charging towards you, step to one side or the other and there you have it, OLE! By doing this, you force the opponent to adjust their direction, which reduces the pressure on you momentarily, allowing you time to apply pressure of your own from a new angle.

This top-down drawing should clear things up for you.

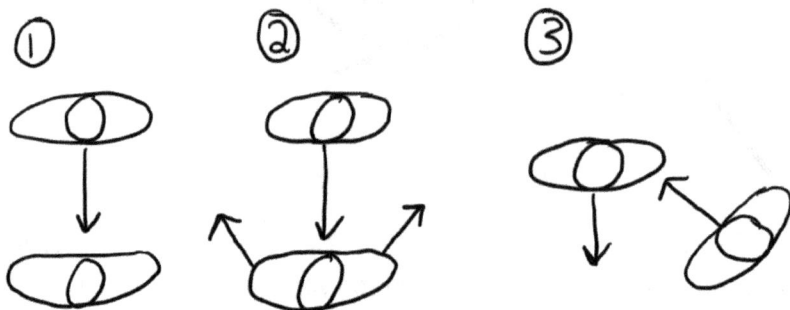

Under it

Going under the pressure will only apply to certain rule sets, as it usually involves taking the opponent to the ground.

In an MMA scenario, if the opponent is running in and trying to punch us in the face, it is often very effective to lower your level and shoot for a double or single-leg takedown. Royce Gracie and Kazushi Sakuraba, amongst many others, were masters of this.

Do you remember me talking about the Harimau Silat guys and how they dropped under the fog earlier? This sort of technique works quite well against heavy forward pressure. On the downside, you have to remember that, as with all techniques, timing is everything. If you are putting your head near their legs, you may be asking for a knee in the face. Fair warning!

Over it

If you can do jumping splits over your opponent's head, then you probably don't need to read this book!

Another situation in which you would go over it is when the opponent applies pressure to your lower body. If they shoot in for a double-leg takedown and you sprawl on top of them, you are going over the pressure.

Stand your ground

This is possibly the hardest one to perform of the six examples. This is where simultaneous attack and defence can be your friend. It requires timing and calmness under pressure. We discussed it in the Five Ways of Defence chapter.

Simultaneous attack and defence works so well because people are very vulnerable when they attack. You don't expect to get hit when you attack, do you? Why would you throw an attack if you thought that? For that reason, people are often unprepared to receive strikes when they are attacking. This may be a parry and punch, a cover and knee or even a cut kick. Hitting them as they hit you may offer you a moment's respite to apply your own pressure or at least allow you to move away and take the pressure off.

The next step is to create drills which practise dealing with pressure in each of these ways. Being proactive against pressure will go a long way to stopping your opponent from scoring a goal...on your face!

APPLICATIONS ON THE PRESSURE SPECTRUM

Now that we know where we are in the pressure spectrum, we can accurately place our techniques where they belong on that line.

Not all techniques fit all pressures. This exercise will help you identify which are super versatile and which are a bit more niche. You can evaluate this using offensive, defensive, and footwork techniques.

For the purpose of explanation, let's have a look at kicking and kneeing.

To me, the rear leg low round kick to the thigh is one of our most versatile kicks. If we apply it to the pressure spectrum, we can see that it works in one way or another throughout the spectrum.

Here's a low kick on the pressure spectrum:

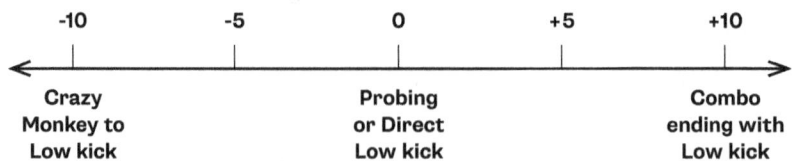

-10	-5	0	+5	+10
Crazy Monkey to Low kick		Probing or Direct Low kick		Combo ending with Low kick

What about a high kick?

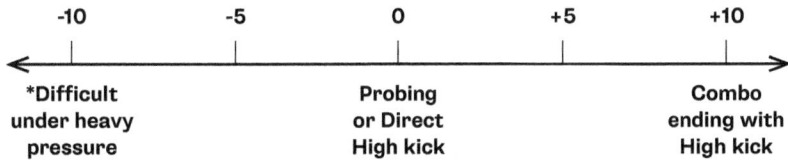

-10	-5	0	+5	+10
*Difficult under heavy pressure		Probing or Direct High kick		Combo ending with High kick

As you can see, the high kick is less useful under heavy pressure. If we throw a high kick when the opponent is rushing us, we risk being off balance and knocked to the floor.

Like many of the other concepts in this book, usefulness in specific pressures will change depending on the rules of your game. In Tae Kwon Do, for example, it doesn't score against you to be pushed to the floor when throwing a high kick under pressure. If it works in your game, add it to the useful pile!

Let's now look at the knee:

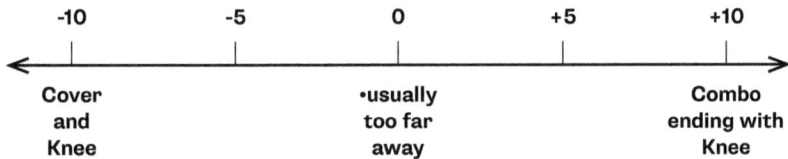

-10	-5	0	+5	+10
Cover and Knee		•usually too far away		Combo ending with Knee

This diagram shows that you are generally too far away to land a knee under neutral pressure, so throwing it at that time may not be the right move.

Now, I'm not saying that these are hard and fast rules. As you know, fighting is incredibly dynamic, and anything can happen, but this will give you a general rule of thumb to work with. Have a look at your favourite attacking techniques and see where they work best on the pressure spectrum.

Now that you understand the idea of offensive techniques on the pressure spectrum, let's group our defensive options in their most applicable pressure category. I will skip positive pressure here because, in that instance, the best defence is a good offence!

Negative pressure

Negative pressure is not the time or place to extend your arms and remove your shields. Keep them close and use your crazy monkey. This pressure is a good time for:

- Cover
- Crazy monkey
- Peek a boo
- Long guard
- Crashing
- Proactive evasion*

*This will depend on the game you are playing. In boxing, you can use preemptive head movement to avoid your opponent's blows, but if your game includes low kicks and knees, it's probably advisable to keep good posture here. This is not the time for reactive evasion unless you live in The Matrix!

Neutral pressure

Neutral pressure allows the time and space for offensive defence. This includes:

- Parrying, scooping and catching
- Simultaneous attack and defence
- Interceptions and stop hits
- Insertions
- Reactive evasion
- Essentially, the more complicated stuff!

Now, I know you are asking, Matt, what else can we map on the pressure spectrum?

Good question! Here is one we used earlier: Let's put the five ways of attack and the five ways of defence on the pressure spectrum. (Would you believe me if I said this drawing came to me in a dream? Ask my wife; she will confirm it!)

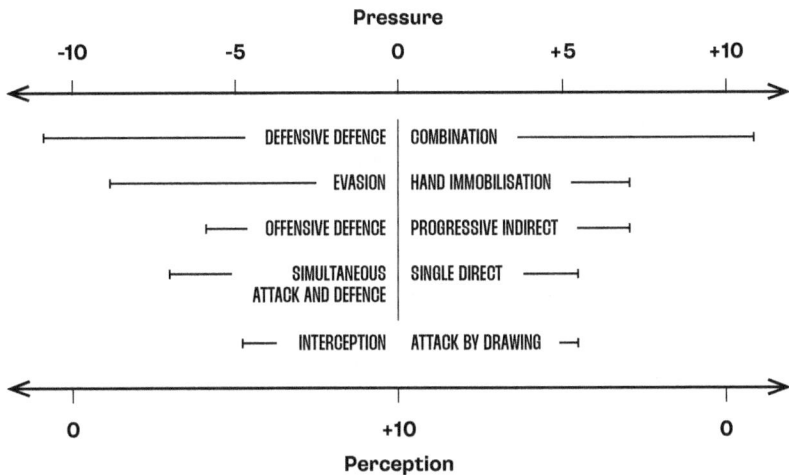

Pressure

| -10 | -5 | 0 | +5 | +10 |

DEFENSIVE DEFENCE | COMBINATION

EVASION | HAND IMMOBILISATION

OFFENSIVE DEFENCE | PROGRESSIVE INDIRECT

SIMULTANEOUS ATTACK AND DEFENCE | SINGLE DIRECT

INTERCEPTION | ATTACK BY DRAWING

| 0 | +10 | 0 |

Perception

As you can see from the top and bottom lines, there is also a correlation between pressure and perception. Generally, the higher the pressure, whether positive or negative, the lower our perception is. This is why it's hard to do complex things under high levels of pressure.

Using the pressure spectrum to analyse your techniques will give you a better idea of what toolbox to open and when.

Pressure will always be a part of martial arts. We must respect it, learn to apply it, and, most importantly, learn to deal with it.

We need to introduce pressure gradually into all of our training. Remember the marathon metaphor? Don't run 26 miles in your first session! Build up the pressure gradually so that you can learn to cope with it without it being overwhelming. Try to spend as little time training in neutral pressure as possible. Neutral pressure is a vacuum, and unfortunately, vacuums don't happen very often in combat.

If you get comfortable under pressure, there will be no stopping you!

NOTES ON THE PRESSURE SPECTRUM:

- **Think of pressure like a soccer field. Are you near their goal? Are they near your goal? Or are you in the middle of the field?**

- **Apply pressure appropriately so you don't throw yourself off balance or expose yourself to counters.**

- **Deal with your opponent's pressure by going away from it, into it, left or right of it, under it, over it, or standing your ground and countering it.**

- **Map where your techniques and tactics are most effective on the pressure spectrum.**

18. TENNIS, ANYONE?

A lot of my childhood was spent around a tennis court. My father was the president of a tennis club and a fantastic player. This club had a magical playground next to it that was every kid's dream. Looking back, it was probably a health and safety nightmare, but we didn't care as we threw ourselves from the gigantic twirly slide onto the mammoth tyres nearby.

Eventually, I drifted from throwing myself around the playground to hitting a few balls around the court as I joined the ranks of the club's junior players.

I'm sure you are wondering at this point what tennis has to do with martial arts. I hear you. When I start explaining this, you will probably have the same look on your face as my students. Bear with me; I shall explain.

Have you ever looked at the stats after watching a tennis match? No, probably not, and I respect that decision! I started to look at them about 15 years ago and was blown away by the discovery. It seems that the person who makes the fewest unforced errors usually wins. It's not always the case, but it definitely seems to affect the game's outcome. Obvious, right?! This directly ties in to the previous chapter on pressure. It seems the better you deal with pressure, the fewer mistakes you make.

I started to think about how this applied to martial arts and how we could define it to help us in our games.

Here are the four ideas I came up with. If you think about it, they are the only things you need to do to win! Easy, right?

DON'T MAKE UNFORCED ERRORS

I told you my dad is a fantastic tennis player, right? Well back when I was a cocky teenager he was incredibly frustrating to play against. He is known in the community as a wall. Whatever you do, the ball always comes back. He never makes a mistake. So frustrating! He lets you make the mistake, and you end up beating yourself. Or he waits for the perfect moment when you are out of position and finishes you off with perfectly timed pressure.

I noticed the exact same thing when sparring with world champions in Muay Thai. They don't make unforced errors, and their cube is impenetrable. It is very difficult to land a direct technique on them.

An unforced error is something you do while not under pressure that creates an opening for your opponent. You can make unforced errors by breaking one or more aspects of your cube.

From a Muay Thai perspective, if you unwittingly have your hand down, you have broken your structure and opened yourself to a punch or kick to the face.

If you lean too far forward, backwards, or to the side, your posture will be corrupted, and you may be exposed to a low-line attack or strike to the body.

Crossing your feet when you move corrupts your base and may allow your opponent a free kick to your leg.

If you can maintain your posture, structure and base, you will reduce unforced errors, thereby limiting the free hits your opponent gets.

CAPITALISE ON THEIR UNFORCED ERRORS

The other side of that coin is that we need to be able to recognise and exploit our opponents' unforced errors. The ability to inherently know when the opponent has made a mistake is a crucial skill that we need to develop.

Of course, this ties into the rules of whatever sport we are fighting in. To give an example from Muay Thai, perhaps your opponent steps too wide or crosses their feet when moving, thus exposing themselves to a low kick they cannot block.

Perhaps your opponent keeps their lead hand very low so you can land a punch where they have broken their structure.

I use the cube to determine where they may be making mistakes. These could be in their structure (hands and arms), posture (head and spine), or base (feet and legs).

Generally, these mistakes are made when the opponent doesn't realise they are breaking their cube or when they get tired. It is much harder to keep a strong cube when we are tired. Usually, the more skilled and more conditioned the opponent is, the less likely they are to break their cube.

DEAL WITH PRESSURE WELL SO YOU DON'T MAKE FORCED ERRORS.

Of course, no sporting endeavour occurs in a vacuum. The opponent will always try to apply pressure, and the better we can hold our cube under this pressure, the less likely we are to make forced errors.

Sometimes, when you watch the best tennis players in the world, it seems like they are just standing in the middle of the court while their opponent runs helplessly from side to side, chasing down balls, desperate to get them back over the net. The great players are unflappable under pressure and focus on getting back to their optimum position as soon as they have hit a shot, therefore making it less likely that they make forced errors.

To improve this ability, we must train against varying degrees of pressure and focus on holding our cube. We must also train ourselves not to flinch or overreact to our opponents' strikes. Flinching and overreacting are forced errors; if our opponent sees it happen, they will capitalise on it.

APPLY APPROPRIATE PRESSURE SO THEY MAKE FORCED ERRORS, BUT YOU DON'T MAKE UNFORCED ONES.

If you are playing tennis against the person who always gets the ball back, and you hit the ball to the middle of the court, you are applying no pressure. This will result in you wearing yourself down, making mistakes, and eventually smashing your racket into the fence in frustration. Of course, I'm not speaking from personal experience!

Against that sort of opponent, you have to vary your shots and move them around the court until they become vulnerable. This is where setups become essential. It is very useful to hit shots that are not necessarily designed to be winners. These shots apply pressure and draw the opponent out of their optimum platform so that you can capitalise on the openings they give you.

The same idea is used in sparring or fighting. Sparring with top practitioners, you soon find out that throwing only positive attacks (attacks meant to be winners) usually gets you nowhere. Their cube is strong, and they can deal with all of it.

We must introduce some negative attacks (shots designed to draw the opponent out) so that we can capitalise on the openings that are given. The better their cube, the harder this is to do and the more setups we need to use. Negative attacks can include progressive indirect attacks and the attack-by-drawing tactics that we discussed in Chapter 11.

On the other hand, we must be careful when applying pressure and avoid exposing ourselves by making unforced errors. Sometimes, if we are too exuberant with our pressure or a little sloppy with our setup, we may pay the price of an unforced error.

So keep your cube and watch your statistics!

NOTES ON TENNIS, ANYONE?

- **Don't make unforced errors.**

- **Deal with pressure so you don't make forced errors.**

- **Capitalise on their unforced errors.**

- **Apply appropriate pressure so they make forced errors, but you don't make unforced ones.**

19. THE RHYTHM IS GONNA GET YOU

Underneath every moment of combat lies a heartbeat, a constant rhythm that keeps time for everything that happens. Whenever I train, I have a metronome ticking away in my head.

TIK-TOK-TIK-TOK-TIK-TOK-TIK-TOK

These beats control the fight. The tempo may be slow when not much is happening, or it can be fast and furious! (Giving it a little more allegro!)

The beats can be empty or contain footwork, striking, defence, faking, feinting, trapping, or grappling. They can be even or broken, and they can even make you a better dancer!

I have heard several ways to categorise these beats. Today, I will give you my version; hopefully, it will help you understand how they work. I use quasi-musical notation, but I must warn you that I know nothing about music, so please forgive me; it is purely for demonstration purposes only! Of course, the descriptions will be accompanied by the usual helpful drawings!

Let's quickly define a whole beat and a half beat. To me, a whole beat sounds like a giant walking towards me DUM DUM DUM DUM. Each DUM is a whole beat. Make sense?

Now picture a magician saying TA-DA! To me, that is one and a half beats. Confused? Ok, try this: on your desk, wall or hand, start a rhythmic tapping about a second apart. DUM DUM DUM; after three of those, do two quick taps in a row, TA-DA. DUM DUM DUM TA-DA DUM DUM DUM TA-DA.

(This is where your partner or kids tell you to put this book down and seek help!)

I hope that makes sense. Let's examine a few defensive rhythms and how we can use them to counter our opponent.

Two beat counter = Block - Hit

A two-beat counter is when the defending and attacking motions are consecutive whole beats. For example, if I parried your right cross with my left hand and threw my right cross back, that would be a two-beat counter.

One-and-a-half beat counter = BlockHit

A one-and-a-half beat counter is when the second motion follows immediately after the first and lands before another whole beat occurs. This is the magicians' TA-DA! This normally happens when your defence is halfway to the target. If I parry your jab with my right hand and shoot a right cross directly from where I parried it to your face, that would be a one and a half beat counter.

Sometimes, I will say that a full beat is block and hit, whereas a half beat is blockhit. Does that make sense? Essentially, the half-beat lands a fraction earlier than the whole beat.

Simultaneous beat counter
= Block and Hit at the same time

Now, with the simultaneous beat counter, the block and hit happen at the same time. This is called simultaneous attack and defence. If you threw your left jab at me, and I parried it with my right hand as I hit you in the face at the same time with my left jab, that would be a simultaneous beat counter.

It may be one of the best ways to stop someone's forward pressure and not let your opponent build momentum in their attack. Also, remember that they are at their most vulnerable when they are striking you, so it is a great time to repay the favour!

Pre-beat = Interception

Pre-beat is a tricky one to classify, but essentially, you hit them before they get to finish their whole beat. If you start to jab me, but I react and jab you before your jab can land, this is an interception. Pre-beat is kinda like mind reading. You need to be able to read body language and pick up on your opponent's intention to be able to do this successfully. Of course, this beat takes the most timing and reaction speed out of all the counters. In fact, Bruce Lee thought so highly of the interception that he named his art after it.

Now, let's look at some of the offensive applications of rhythm.

Two (or more) beat attacks = Hit - Hit - Hit

If I throw a left jab and a right cross, that would be a two-beat attack. If I throw a left jab, right cross, left hook, and right kick combo, that would be a four-beat attack sequence.

One and a half beat attacks = HitHit

Typically, a half-beat attack occurs with the same side of your body forward as the initial whole beat. You could even say that both the whole and the following half-beat occur on the same body rotation. For example, if I threw two flicky jabs out without retracting my arm all the way, that would be a half-beat. Or if I threw a left jab, right cross, followed immediately with a right kick on the same body rotation as the cross, this would be a two-and-a-half-beat attack or DUM, TA-DA!

The cool thing is that if you can get your opponent accustomed to whole beats, you can then start to confuse them by breaking that rhythm. For instance, if you introduce an empty beat into your combo, you might bait the opponent into defending something that isn't there, after which you can follow up with another whole beat. Imagine if I threw a left jab; my shoulders would then be oriented to suggest I was about to throw a right cross next. Instead of throwing the cross, I could fake it, thereby leaving that beat empty. If the opponent reacts to that empty beat, I could surprise them with a left hook on the next whole beat.

By mixing up your fighting rhythms, you will keep your opponent guessing when you will launch the next attack. This will keep them mentally off-balance, making it harder for them to build momentum in their offence. Give it a try!

NOTES ON THE RHYTHM:

- **Fighting rhythm exists in all combat as beats.**

- **Beats can be fast or slow, depending on the tempo of the fight.**

- We can use whole beats, half beats, simultaneous beats and pre-beats against our opponent.

- Mix up your rhythms to keep your opponent guessing.

20. HERE COMES THE SCIENCE BIT

So, here's a confession. I was terrible at school. Much to my parents' dismay, I drifted away from formal education as my love for martial arts took over, and I saw it as a potential full-time occupation. Once, I managed a stunning 13% on a physics exam. I probably only scored that well because I got my name correct!

My physics teacher and I never saw eye to eye. He was a practical man teaching practical things, and I was an emotional teenager who thought he knew it all. "Three minutes is not a very long time," he tried to assure us; my reply was, "Well, sir, you have never been in a boxing ring". Zing, wow, I cringe now, looking back. Also, with hilarious irony, I see now that martial arts is physics. Everything we do is physics. Stupid kid.

Nowadays, I love studying the science of fighting. It is the one thing that binds us all together, no matter what style, art, or sport we practise. In this chapter, I want to whet your appetite by giving you a couple of the most prevalent principles that we use at the gym.

One of my students is world-renowned physicist Professor Barry Gallacher. For years, Barry has diligently tried to explain these highly complex principles to me, expanding my knowledge of the "how" of martial arts.

For your sake and mine, dear reader, I will keep these ideas to a workable level. My understanding is at a toddler's level compared to Barry's, so I will do my best to interpret them for you. I feel there is no need to get a PhD in physics to master martial arts, although I suppose it wouldn't hurt.

I also want to say that any errors in this chapter are completely my fault.

F =MA

Ok, guys and gals, we are going to start with the basics. This equation is the one we all learned at school: force equals mass times acceleration. Otherwise known as Newton's second law, this equation is one way to let us know how much force we are generating in our strikes. M represents how much of our mass we can apply, and A represents how fast we can apply it.

When your coach tells you to twist into your punch or turn your hip over when you kick, they are trying to maximise the amount of M you are applying in your strike. Once you can get all of your body behind a strike, you just need to do it super-fast, and you will have a forceful attack.

DEFORMATION VS TRANSLATION OR ROTATION

This principle relates to the first one. At my gym, I categorise our force output into these two groups. Essentially, deformation is a hit, and translation (rotation) is a push. When you hit the heavy bag, does it bow in the middle, or does it swing to the ceiling? If it bows, it's deformation, and if it swings, it's more likely translation (rotation). You may have noticed that I am putting (rotation) after the word translation. This is because this push could rotate something as well as displace it. Have you ever watched a professional wrestler perform a clothesline move? If you haven't, let me explain! It's when they bounce off the ropes and strike their opponent with a straight arm right across the neck. And when the wrestler's head snaps back and their legs fly up in the air, it's a fantastic example of rotation in action! The rotation can occur vertically, horizontally or anywhere in between.

This idea is more in-depth than F=MA as it takes into account our time on target as well. We can express it like this

F x t = m(V2-V1)

F = force
t = time
m = mass
V1 = initial velocity before applying F
V2 = final velocity after applying F for a time (t)

Let's imagine that you are going to hit a heavy bag. In the first instance, you wind up and hit the heavy bag with a big pushing hit. The bag swings. This is often called translation (rotation).

In this case, the F was large, and the t was large. The time your fist was on the target was relatively long. This means the strike was more of a push than a punch. F x t can be large from a push, and the heavy bag is just changing its velocity and swinging.

Okay, now you are going to whack that heavy bag and deliver your energy quickly without pushing. The bag will most likely bow in the middle but not swing that much. This is what we refer to as deformation. Instead of moving the target, it deforms it. Fortunately, all of the things we aim to hit are deformable, i.e. the bag or your opponent's stomach!

With deformation, the F is still large, but the t is small. This means that the time your fist is on the target is less than the translation (rotation) strike. In short, the longer your weapon is on the target when you introduce your force, the more of a push it will be.

Both of these ideas are important. If your goal is to hurt someone, you need less time on target with your strike to achieve deformation. But if you want to corrupt someone's posture, structure, or base to set something else up, you will need more time on target to generate translation or rotation. Being able to distinguish between the two and knowing which to perform when is an excellent skill to have.

FORCE COUPLE

I want to talk about Karate Kid 2. Can you remember that little drum that held all the secrets to fighting? This drum is called den-den daiko. It's a little hand-held drum with a stick coming out of one end. It has two bits of string with beads on the end attached to the side of the drum. As you twist the stick in your hand, these beads hit the drum on alternating sides.

I mention this because the drum represents the rotational mechanics of our shoulders and hips as we perform our techniques. I think the drum illustrates the idea of a force couple quite nicely! I know you are probably thinking, "What the heck is going on here, Matt? Drums, really?" You have come this far, so stick with me just a little longer!

Here is a diagram of our force couple. Because we are (generally) symmetrical beings with two shoulders and two hips on the sides of our bodies, we can generate a lot of our force rotationally. We can maximise this rotational force by pulling and pushing at the same time with opposite sides of our bodies.

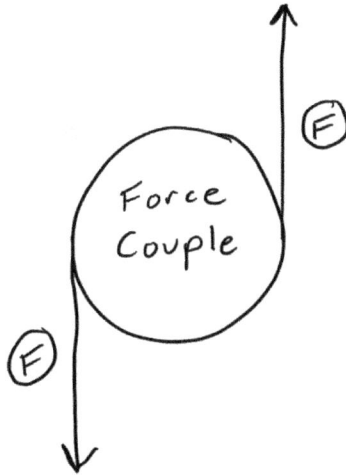

As you can see, the force going in one direction is amplified by the force going in the opposite direction.

An example of this is when you throw a jab cross. To maximise the power of your cross, you must pull your jab back quickly and on the same rotational plane as your cross is going out on. This is one reason why your coach will tell you to bring your guarding hand to your chin when you punch or kick. Everything we do that is rotational should have a push and pull. Next time you throw a punch, kick, knee, or elbow, have a look at the side that isn't hitting. Is it doing its job to maximise your force?

A force couple can be used on a single technique or combination of techniques. I categorise multiple rotations into three groups: Alternating body mechanics, repetitive body mechanics and double body mechanics

Here are some top-down drawings to help you see the concept:

Alternating body mechanics – Jab, Cross

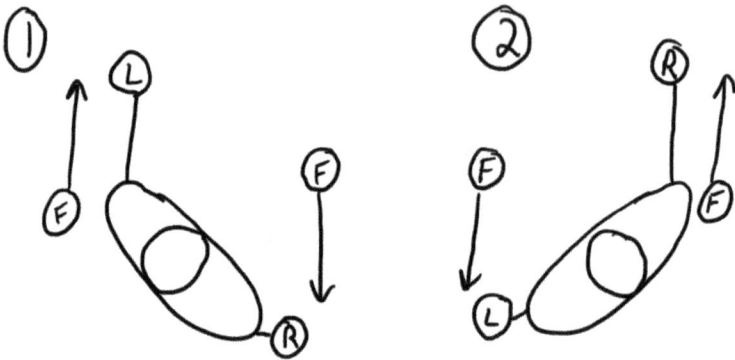

Alternating body mechanics uses alternating sides of the body to generate power. (Not just a clever name!) This is generally the most economical way to strike. This particular sequence has two beats and contains two hits.

Repetitive Body Mechanics – Jab, Lead hook

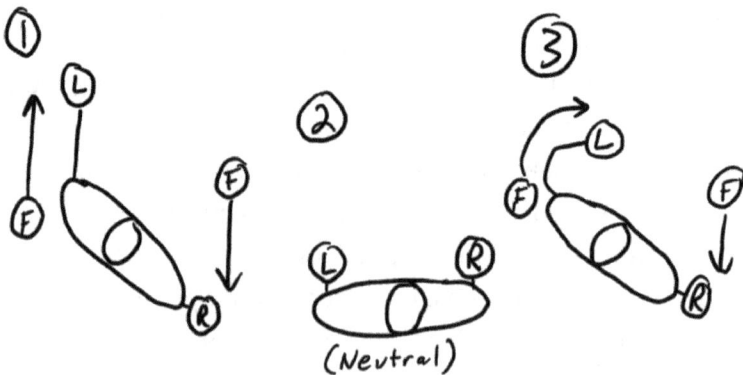

Repetitive body mechanics use the same side of the body to hit multiple times. In order to do this, we have to reload the body to be able to hit with power on the next strike. You can see in this diagram that after the jab, we return to a neutral position so that we can launch another powerful attack. This mechanic is less efficient as it has three motions but only contains two hits. But, repetitive body mechanics are great for deception. People often don't expect two hits coming from the same side. You can also dress up that empty beat with a fake or a feint to really keep your opponent guessing!

Double Body Mechanics
Double body mechanics happen when you perform two hits on the same body rotation. In this example, we are going to throw a jab, cross and rear kick.

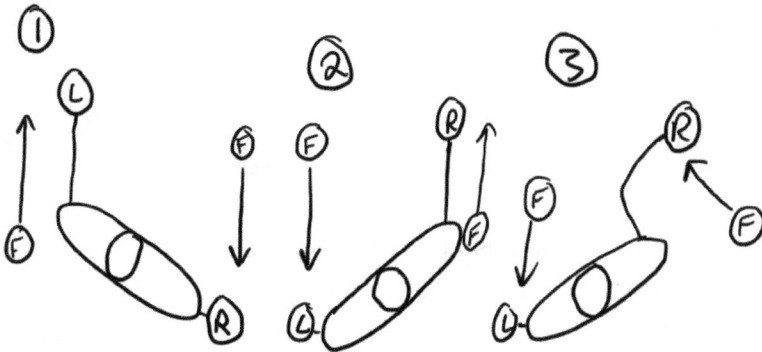

Here, you can see that the second motion (the cross) and the third motion (the kick) occur on the same body rotation. The issue with this mechanic is that there is only so much force you can generate with one body rotation. That means you won't have 100% power on both techniques. You will have 100% to distribute between the two. This is what makes double body mechanics great for setting up powerful shots with distractions. If I use my cross as a distraction, it may only need 10% power to be convincing. This leaves 90% for the kick to smash home!

You can mix and match your body mechanics depending on your goals. Alternating body mechanics is the optimal choice if you want to hit with power. If you want to be sneaky and set something up with distraction and deception, try using repetitive or double body mechanics.

HICK'S LAW

$$RT = a + b \log_2(n)$$

Response Time	Time not involved in decision making	Cognitive processing time per option	Number of alternative

Hick's law describes how our reaction time is affected by the number of possible options available to us. Please don't ask me to explain the equation above. (Remember, I flunked out of physics class!)

From a martial arts perspective, we can boil it down to this: the more possible stimuli you have and the more possible responses to those stimuli you have, the longer your reaction time will be. (I realise that doesn't make scientific sense, but roll with me on this!) Sometimes, we use the term technique log jam. This is when there are too many options, our brain gets overwhelmed, and we often end up doing nothing.

If someone were to kick me in the body, and I only knew one counter to that kick, it would take me very little time to choose my defence. However, if I had ten possible defences, it would take my brain longer to select the correct option.

The bottom line is that the more options you have, the longer the selection process takes. It's like Christmas when you get a huge tin of Quality Street in your stocking. In the beginning, you are rooting around in there for ages to find the coconut one, the elusive purple one, or the caramel one that breaks your teeth. When you are at the bottom with only a few left, you are straight in to nab anything that is left!

This is why fighters train a specific set of techniques for a match. This means they have fewer decisions to make in the ring, thereby reducing their reaction time. While it's okay to know a wide variety of techniques, it's also smart to focus on your preferred ones when you fight so that you don't face too many choices that will slow your reaction time down.

What is the downside to this? Wouldn't it be great if we only had to learn one thing? Unfortunately, this would leave us somewhat vulnerable if that one thing didn't pan out. So we need to have enough selection to cover all our bases, but not so many that we turn into a frozen statue trying to decide what to do.

We can improve our reaction time through training and fitness. If we are tired, it is very difficult to make the right choice.

There are many, many more principles we could include in this chapter, but I wanted to avoid you falling asleep! There are some fantastic books out there, specifically on the science of martial arts. It's worth delving into scientific principles, if only to help you better understand how your techniques work.

NOTES ON THE SCIENCE BIT:

- Maximise force by using more of your mass faster.

- Time on target will determine translation (rotation) or deformation. Translation or rotation is a push, and deformation is a strike.

- Couple your force by pushing and pulling at the same time in opposite directions.

- The more stimuli there are, and the more responses to those stimuli there are, the longer your reaction time will be.

21. ABSORB WHAT IS USEFUL

You probably already know this, but one of Bruce Lee's most famous quotes is: "absorb what is useful". The full quote actually has four parts to it, and they are all invaluable to your progression as a martial artist. Let us explore them together!

Absorb what is useful

How on earth do we know what is useful if we are just starting out? That's a tough question, but the answer is we don't!

When we learn something new, we need to understand it thoroughly before we can decide whether it is useful. We have to try it, test it, and train it in all the ways we can. This process can take months or even years. Once you have thoroughly tested it, you can decide whether it is useful to you right now. If it feels good, pop it in the useful toolbox.

Some things may not be very useful to you as you start out because you don't yet have the attributes to make them work.

Yet is the operative word here. This is why I think it is a great idea to keep notes of all the techniques, tactics and training methods you learn. Even if they aren't useful to you now, they may become so in the future.

Conversely, we must monitor our training as we age, become injured, or change attributes. Some things that may have been useful to you in the past may now be useless.

On a side note, if you are thinking of becoming a coach, it's a great idea to keep that notepad handy. Even if something is useless to you, it may be very useful to some of your students.

Reject what is useless

I'm always very careful about rejecting techniques, tactics, or training methods. You have to give them a fair trial run before putting them into long-term storage. Try them over and over in training, and if you feel you are getting nowhere and if they are of no value to you at the moment, then relinquish them to storage to possibly be revived later in your journey. It is also important to take them out of storage every now and then, dust them off, and see if they fit yet. I did the same thing with olives! Man, when I was young, I hated olives. But on a recent trip to Italy, I was convinced to give it another go. Turns out I like olives now. Just like techniques, you may not hate olives forever!

Research your own experience

It's very easy to fall into the trap of only listening to what other people say. In the beginning, this is normal because you don't have much of your own experience to draw from. As you spend more and more time training you will start to form your own conclusions on what works for you. I'm always making mental notes on what has worked for me and what hasn't, what I did well and what I need to improve.

I recently installed some heaters on the ceiling of our reception room at the gym. On the same day, I saw one of the students run through and put his hand under the cold tap. "What happened?" I said. He replied, "I wanted to know where that heat was coming from, so I touched the heater." It made sense at the time, right? We have all been there. But I will guarantee he won't do it again as he has looked at his experience, drawn conclusions from it and made a plan not to touch it again!

So, in your martial arts training, it will really benefit you to start analysing your experiences and results. Think about those results and why they occurred. Then, you can start making plans to improve where you can. Your experiences can be your best learning tool if you learn to listen to them! And please don't touch heaters!

Add what is specifically your own

It takes a certain degree of competence to reach this point, but it will become increasingly important as your knowledge of the art grows.

With enough experience, you will begin to "create" new things that you can apply in your sparring or fighting. Now, I have put the word create in the inverted commas, and I want you to imagine me doing them in the air as I say it. I have done this because, more than likely, you haven't created it.

But in a way, you have "created" it. (Again, imagine me doing air quotes.) It's probable that someone, somewhere in the history of the world, has done it before you, but that's OK because the main thing here is that you discovered it on your own. This means your understanding of the game is so deep that internal education becomes possible.

People sometimes come into the gym and tell me they were self-taught. Personally, I think this is impossible. Imagine trying to teach a toddler to read by putting them in a room with a load of books and saying, off you go!

What they probably mean is that they didn't have formal training. They learned from videos, books, or from their mates in their garage, which is not the same as teaching yourself. But once you have enough knowledge and understanding, you will be able to make discoveries on your own!

NOTES ON THE ABSORB WHAT IS USEFUL:

- **Absorb what is useful.**

- **Reject what is useless.**

- **Research your own experiences**

- **Add what is specifically your own.**

22. LEARNING AND DEVELOPMENT

I'm going to cram two ideas into this chapter, if that's okay with you. They are related, and they both have five steps, so I think they will fit nicely here!

Determining where you are on your journey is vital to figuring out where to go next. Here are two ways to do that. The first five focus more on the physical aspects of fighting, while the second five deal more with mental and psychological development.

FIVE PHASES OF DEVELOPMENT

I learned this from my coach, Johan Skalberg. I use it in my curricula now, as I feel it's a great way to assess one's physical development.

I call these the five stages of learning. They are:

- **Primitive**
- **Technical**
- **Mechanical**
- **Flow**
- **Creative**

I've used the jab as an example to illustrate this, but you can use these phases of learning for any and all of your techniques.

Primitive

This is when you are learning the very basics of the technique. You are at the stage where you know the jab is a lead straight punch, but not much more than that. The punch may or may not go straight to the target, and it may or may not come straight back to your chin. Also, more than likely, the guarding hand is not present yet. But please don't worry, the technical phase is just around the corner!

Technical

In the technical phase, you can now throw a jab that starts at your chin and returns to your chin in a straight line. You also know that your other hand is up and guarding your head. All of the technical parts of the jab are coming together nicely.

Mechanical

If you are in the mechanical phase, you are now throwing the jab with your body behind it. You are on the ball of your foot, twisting your knees, hips, and shoulders to develop more power. You are starting to understand how your body works as a whole to develop power.

Flow

After completing the previous three, you can add the jab to the flow. You can throw it at the beginning or the end of a sequence. Sometimes, it flows out right in the middle. Your jab is now silky smooth, and you know it!

Creative

The world is your lobster! You can now use the jab to fake, feint, or distract the opponent so you can land something else. You can smash with it or draw with it. It has become your paintbrush.

Once you fully understand the technique, it becomes like Lego; you can use it however you want.

So, next time you train, consider your performance. Where are you in the learning process? What do you need to improve to advance to the next phase? Always moving onwards and upwards!

THE FIVE STAGES OF LEARNING

Another interesting way we can monitor our progress through our training is with the five stages of learning. Initially, there were four stages, but the powers-that-be have decided to add another. These stages are:

1. **Unconscious incompetence.**
2. **Conscious incompetence.**
3. **Conscious competence.**
4. **Unconscious competence.**
5. **Conscious, unconscious competence.**

Unconscious incompetence
Basically, this is when you don't know how bad you are! Probably a slightly nicer way of saying that is you don't know what you don't know. This is the stage of innocence where we stumble into a new world, not knowing what to expect. You might go into it thinking you have an idea of what's going on, only to be completely blown away by how vast the topic actually is. I love that moment!

Conscious incompetence

Crap, I've just realised how bad I am at all of this and how big this topic really is. This normally goes one of two ways. Either people get overwhelmed and quit, or they dig in and use that feeling as motivation to become better.

I remember trying to learn the Thai language to help me understand the coaches better when I was training in Thailand. I started with the basics and was going great guns until I realised it was a whole language! It is going to take me years and years to become any good at this. Hmm, I thought, how often am I in Thailand anyway? Actually, I think those language CDs are still in the loft!

When we try to do something, we need motivation and inspiration to overcome the effort required to achieve it. But if we do stick at it, we will pass into...

Conscious competence

Now, we are getting somewhere! You are becoming really good and are being rewarded with lots of praise, promotions, trophies, medals, and wins! You can perform all of the techniques independently, but you may still have to focus to do so. The downside to this stage is that sometimes your ego can overtake your humility.

Unconscious competence

You are the Zen master. You don't punch; your fist hits all by itself. You do your techniques without having to think about them. This level is for those who have put in the long, hard years of training. These people have gained what they call tacit knowledge. That is the knowledge we gain through experience that we can't explain. This is what distinguishes this level from the next one.

Conscious, unconscious competence

Now, you can explain how you do what you do. These people are the coaches of the world. They have an innate ability to do things and can share how they do them.

So you see what I mean when I say that martial arts don't really start paying off until you have a couple of decades of experience under your black belt!

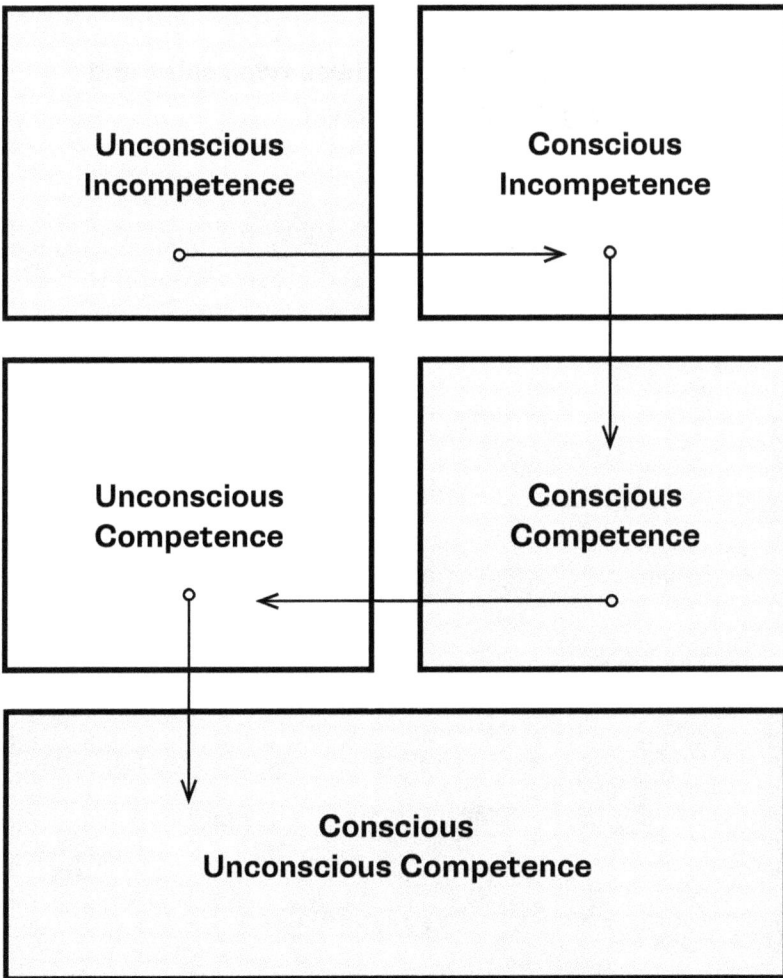

```
┌──────────────────────┐  ┌──────────────────────┐
│                      │  │                      │
│     Unconscious      │  │      Conscious       │
│    Incompetence      │  │    Incompetence      │
│          o───────────┼──┼──────────→ o         │
│                      │  │            │         │
└──────────────────────┘  └────────────┼─────────┘
                                        │
┌──────────────────────┐  ┌────────────┼─────────┐
│                      │  │            ↓         │
│     Unconscious      │  │      Conscious       │
│     Competence       │  │     Competence       │
│          o ←─────────┼──┼──────────o           │
│          │           │  │                      │
└──────────┼───────────┘  └──────────────────────┘
           │
┌──────────┼───────────────────────────────────────┐
│          ↓                                        │
│                    Conscious                      │
│           Unconscious Competence                  │
│                                                   │
└───────────────────────────────────────────────────┘
```

NOTES ON LEARNING AND DEVELOPMENT:

- **The five phases of development are Primitive, Technical, Mechanical, Flow, and Creative.**

- **The five stages of learning are: unconscious incompetence, conscious incompetence, conscious competence, unconscious competence, conscious unconscious competence.**

- **Evaluate your progress on these two scales and plan how to get to the next level.**

23. BE A GOOD BAD GUY

Sounds like a paradox, right?

When your training partner is working their stuff on you, you are now the Bad Guy. So being a good bad guy means you are the best training partner you can be. Over the years, I have seen many different types of training partners. Please believe me when I say that not all are created equal.

BE SOMEONE PEOPLE WANT TO TRAIN WITH

The golden rule of martial arts is to train unto others as you would have them train unto you. That makes sense, right? I hope so because I just made it up!

Be the training partner you would like to train with. It takes a while to get the hang of this. You need to have some degree of competence before giving someone else what they need. As you progress, you will become a caring and empathetic training partner who will go out of your way to help your partner get better. Then, they, in turn, will do the same for you. Win-win!

Selfish training partners are very difficult to work with. They only think of their progress and how they will benefit from the training. These people tend to train on people, not with them. Eventually, nobody wants to train with them, as their ego is too much to deal with. They often end up hurting people just to prove how good they are.

To help with that problem at our gym, I use the analogy of one tribe.

In the old days, tribes had to train together before they went out to fight the enemy. It was their tribe against everyone else, so they had to train very cleverly. They had to make everyone as good as possible without anyone getting hurt, because if they did, their tribe would be a team member down when they went to fight their opponents.

So, at our gym, we are one tribe. We train together to improve everyone's performance because your tribe is only as strong as your weakest link.

Next time your coach says, "Grab a training partner," look around your gym. It's interesting to see who everyone runs to train with and who they avoid. If you want to get the most out of your training, be the person everyone wants to train with. I can guarantee that people will give you their best if you are.

YOU SMELL

You do. I do. We all do sometimes, some more than others, right?! If you think you don't smell sometimes when you are training, it's because the people around you are polite!

You can always see the involuntary facial twitch as someone is partnered with the odorous person in class, no matter how hard they try to hide it.

I have seen many different ways to deal with this problem. Some are subtle, and some are not so subtle.

Some coaches leave a deodorant can in the locker room with a sign on the wall indicating that everyone should use it. Some coaches just embarrass the person by telling them they stink in front of the class. I have even seen someone hang car air fresheners in and around someone's locker.

I usually just walk past the offending student and whisper in their ear that their t-shirt might need a wash. Hint, hint, hint! It's not you; it's the t-shirt. (PS It's you!)

These instances can all be avoided by turning up for class washed and deodorised with clean clothes and breath. One person I knew even liberally doused himself with baby powder before class. You always knew where he had been on the mats!

Being a good training partner includes being as inoffensive on the nose as possible!

DIRTY HABITS

Okay, here is a checklist of things I have seen people do that make for unpleasant training partners. (And just generally, actually!) If you do any of these things (you dirty mucker), now's the time to improve them.

- Do you have a running nose and wipe it with your hand or arm?
- Do you have a running nose and wipe it on your t-shirt?
- Do you blow your nose in your t-shirt? (Uggg)
- Do you spit into your t-shirt? (Yep)
- Do you spit anywhere other than in a private bathroom?
- Do you pick your nose, crotch or bottom while training?
- Do you pick spots, scabs or cold sores while training?

- Are you bleeding from anywhere?
- Are you sick?
- Did you eat fish, onions or garlic before training?
- Do your t-shirts, gloves or shin pads have mould on them?
- Do you have verrucas (warts) on your feet?
- Do you have long fingernails or toenails?

Yeah, I know, right. Folks have some funny habits! Figure out what yours are and make training pleasant for your partner!

COMMUNICATE

Probably the most important ability as a training partner is being able to communicate. It's normal in martial arts to let our egos or preconceptions get in the way of explaining what we need. We don't want to look weak. We should be able to suck it up and take it. Or even worse, maybe we can't take it, and we won't be returning to training.

I always ask my classes, "If your training partner is hitting you too hard, whose fault is it?" The training partner's? Nope, it's yours. Unless they are doing it maliciously, how do they know if they are hitting you too hard? We all have very different thresholds for pain and stress. And while they may change over time, it's important to let our partners know what you are okay dealing with now.

By the same token, it's important to let your partner know if you want them to work harder on you. If things are too light and slow, you won't grow, so you need to tell your partner to amp it up! Talking to your partner will help you find that sweet spot training point where you are ever so slightly outside your comfort zone but not so far as to put you off.

STUDENT COACHES

Another interesting thing I see almost every day is the student teacher. Often, a student with very little experience will coach another student with slightly less experience. Or even better, a student with very little experience coaching another student with more experience than them! I appreciate that it comes from a good place, but often, what they are showing someone is wrong and often done in a way that won't help. Coaches have honed their skills of getting information across for years; use them! If you are in any way unsure if your partner is doing it right, grab a coach and get them to have a look!

BE WHAT YOUR TRAINING PARTNER NEEDS YOU TO BE

This skill will take some time and experience, but it's definitely worth aiming for. As a coach, whenever I train someone, I ask myself who they need me to be right now to benefit most from this session.

For instance, I have three levels when I hold pads for a Muay Thai class: basic, hybrid and advanced.

In the basic feed, I hold the pad, and they hit it. This simple call-and-response style of feeding is great for new students.

The hybrid feed is the same as the basic feed, but I also encourage the students to throw certain things whenever they like, regardless of what I am currently holding for them. So now it is part call and response and part self-initiation.

The advanced pad feed is essentially a sparring session with the terminator. The student throws whatever they want, and I get the pad there for them to hit.

My job is to figure out what the student I am working with

needs at that moment and which level will benefit them.

When I worked with my fighters, I often tried to become the person they were fighting. Was their opponent a southpaw? I had to become a southpaw. Were they grapplers who just wanted to take them down? That's what I would try to do.

You can even take this idea across to self-defence. Who are you training to defend yourself against? If you are training to defend against a drunk guy who just wants to beat you up, then it won't help if your partner acts like a Muay Thai fighter. They have to act like a drunk guy who just wants to beat you up!

So, when you are next training, and it's your partner's turn, think about what they might need you to be. When it's your turn, make sure you also communicate to your partner what you need them to be. That way, you will both get the most out of your training time together.

So, in summary, to be a good training partner, you have to be a good, bad guy!

NOTES ON BEING A GOOD, BAD GUY:

- Be the training partner people want to work with.

- Take care of your personal hygiene and habits.

- Talk to your partner. If they are going too hard, tell them. If they are going too soft, tell them.

- Unless you are qualified or sure you are right, try not to teach others.

- Think about what your training partner needs from you. Let them know what you need from them.

24. AGEING IN MARTIAL ARTS

We are fast approaching the end of this book, and I want to thank you for sticking with me thus far! Since we are nearing the finish line, I want to examine ageing in martial arts.

One thing that saddens me is seeing people who have a passion for fighting quit martial arts after their fighting career is over. When these fighters finish training after their five- or so-year run, I want to say, "Noooooo, don't stop. The journey is just beginning. There is so much more to this thing than fighting." I truly believe that it takes 10, 15, or even 40 years for the real benefits of martial arts to reveal themselves.

I know that's a weird statement, but it's true. The longer you are in the martial arts world, the less it becomes about "fighting". Of course, it's still all about fighting at its core, but as you age, it becomes more about learning, training and coaching. It becomes about keeping your body and your brain active in an incredibly diverse way.

My coach, Ron, would give me advice when I hit certain birthdays:

"OK, Matt, now that you are in your 20s, you can expect this from your training and your body."

Or

"Now that you are in your 30s, you should be training like this."

This advice is so important because adapting how we train as we age allows us to keep our passion for martial arts alive!

Ron's coach is Dan Inosanto, who is still training and teaching in his late 80s at the time of this writing! I have seen several older masters perform incredible things. They keep going and learning and find joy in passing what they know on to the generations that follow them. This is what keeps them alive and youthful.

I aim to become one of those old, grizzled coaches who need a cane to get on the mats, but once there, they explode into action like Yoda fighting Count Dooku!

THREE STAGES OF TRAINING

One question often overlooked in martial arts is: when will this training benefit me? We are usually concerned with instant gratification and how this thing we are doing will help us right now. We aren't normally concerned with how it will help us in 20 years.

But now that you are going to be a lifelong martial artist, I want you to think about your training in three stages:

Short-term training

This is all the heavy-going stuff that will give us results quickly: smashing pads, hard sparring, intense grappling, full-contact stick fighting, and even heavy weight training. These are all great to train and are super fun, but they do take their toll on your body and mind. This is certainly a younger person's game.

Mid-term training

Mid-term training is when we begin to think ahead. What will we need 15 years down the line? This is really difficult because when you're 20, how often do you engage in activities that will benefit your 40-year-old self? I know I didn't do much to help that future version of myself, that's for certain!

Mid-term training involves drilling, lighter technical sparring, relaxed rolling, and body weight exercises.

As we age, we tend to gravitate toward these methods anyway because our bodies find ultra-heavy sessions harder to endure and harder to recover from. If you start martial arts in your 40s or later, you probably want to start here because if you start in the short-term training category, you run a much higher risk of injury if your body isn't ready for that kind of abuse.

This is more like a massage than sparring!

Long term training

Have you ever watched an old-timer football game or a senior tennis tournament? Sure, they don't move as fast as they once did, and their power is less than it was, but what is super cool to me is that they are still doing it! Can I still do the thing I love doing even when I am old? The answer is yes if you train smart. Long-term training includes energy drills, lighter pad work, flow sparring, gentle rolling, yoga, force manipulation, mind control and levitation!

Ummmm

Now, I totally understand that you won't always think about these stages. I know I didn't, especially when I was younger. But it's something to keep in mind as you progress through your training. You'll thank me when you are 50!

Unfortunately, there will come a time when you will have to slow down. It's important at this stage not to compare your current self to your younger self. When you are 50 you may not be able to do what you could when you were 20, and that's ok. I have seen many people quit martial arts because they couldn't do what they used to be able to do. While this realisation is very disheartening, as long as you keep learning, growing, and training smart, you can continue to participate in your passion forever!

Training stage as it relates to age

In your teens and twenties, you will probably spend 90% of your time on short-term training and 10% on mid- to long-term training.

This will shift as you enter your 30s and 40s. It could be closer to 50% short-term and 50% mid- and long-term training.

When you reach your 50s and beyond, you will find that a more significant portion of your training will drift into the mid- to long-term stage as you preserve your body and brain.

Obviously, this will be different for everyone. I mean, goodness me, Dan the Beast Severn was still fighting in MMA when he was 53! But for the most part, the miles do add up, and even if they do, there is always something you can do to keep your training going and preserve your love of martial arts!

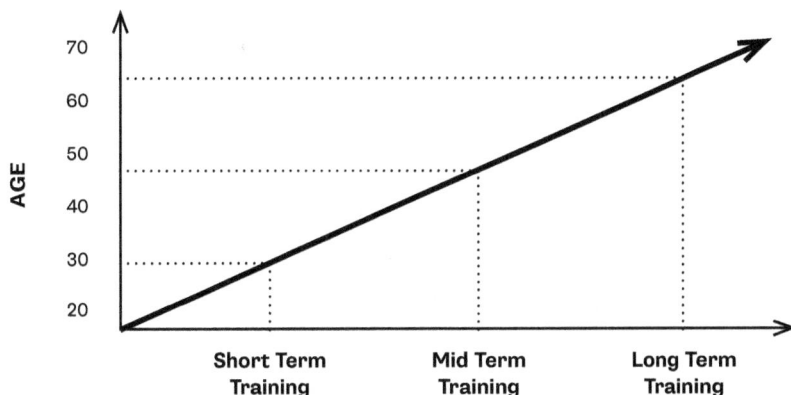

MASTERY

Have you read Malcolm Gladwell's book Outliers? It's a very cool book! If you haven't read it yet, add it to your list.

One of the fundamental ideas he presents in that book is mastery. He discusses why great people are great, arguing that the right person, at the right moment in time, with the right amount of practice, could become an outlier. That is my understanding in a nutshell, of course.

The magic number is 10,000 hours. Train for that long, and you will become a master. Give or take a few hours here or there!

I personally prefer 36,000,000 seconds. I wonder how much of our training hours are spent actually training? That's okay; you are allowed to chat, but we have to account for it.

Think about it. At your current training rate, how long will it take you to become a master? To reach that unconscious competence stage? Adding one or two extra hours a week will make a big difference!

One hour a week for ten years will earn you 520 hours, while three hours a week for ten years will earn you 1560 hours. That's a big difference, right?

What about over 20 years?

One hour per week = 1040 hours

Three hours per week = 3120 hours

Six hours per week = 6240 hours

Now we are getting in sight of that 10,000 hours!

I know - it's a long slog. There are a lot of ups and downs, but you are doing this for the journey, not the destination, right? You will get there before you know it, and when you do, you will look back on the journey with a big smile on your face! Remember, a day in the game is worth a year of memories!

And don't worry if you won't make it that far. It's totally okay not to make it to mastery, too. This is your journey, so you do it for your reasons! Make your martial arts journey your own. You get as much or as little as you want from it, but if you love it, just keep going! As coach Yoda says, "Do or do not. There is no try!"

KNOWLEDGE VS PHYSICAL ABILITIES

So, with any luck, we will all get old. Sorry about that. But one fantastic thing about martial arts is that much of it is knowledge-based. This is the side of martial arts that can be beneficial even when you can't do the hard training anymore.

I find myself drifting more toward this side of martial arts the older I get. The history of the arts, how they migrated, the culture of the people, and what made them create their style in the first place are of much greater interest to me now than when I was in my twenties.

I love to break things down more now and figure out why they work and what structure suits what rule set. I drive my wife crazy with this stuff, wandering around the house muttering about martial arts all the time. She finds folded-up notes with undecipherable lists of techniques and ideas in all of my pockets and desk drawers.

I feel very secure with the knowledge that even if my body can't do what it could years ago, or if there comes a day when I can't train, I will still have some value to share through my knowledge of the arts.

Physical ability vs knowledge graph

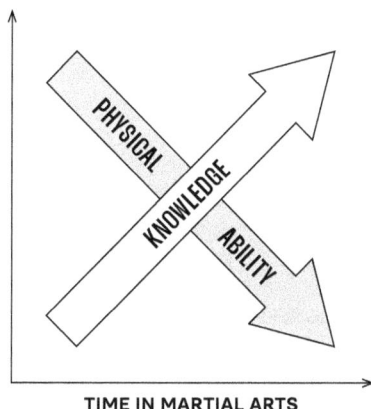

TIME IN MARTIAL ARTS

INTENSITY AND CONSISTENCY

One of the toughest things I have ever had to do in the martial arts is to admit I can't train like I used to. While it's fun to try and keep up with the young folks in the gym, it takes its toll more and more every year, and if I'm honest, it bothered me that I was slipping. Nobody wants to get old and have their body wear down. Along with the physical deterioration, I started to notice a physiological trend in older people. It seems their inner coach tells them that if they can't do martial arts in the way they could when they were younger, then there is no point in doing it at all. That is something that I definitely didn't want to happen to me. I love martial arts, I don't want to quit them, but I can't sustain this training anymore. What do I do?

Here's what I found to be the tricky part: we as martial artists find it very hard to permit ourselves to take it easier. We have been trained from day one to keep going, show no pain, do more, work harder, keep fighting, never give up no matter what, no mercy sensei oouuusss! We don't learn how to take it easy, and we certainly don't want to look weak.

I think that as we get to a point when we find it hard to keep up, we have to give ourselves permission to go easier. Tough choice, I know, but if it's that or giving up, I know which one I'll choose!

A nice way to frame that is with the intensity vs consistency graph.

When we are young, we want the consistency and intensity of our workouts to be high. At this point, our bodies can take it and we can grow exponentially.

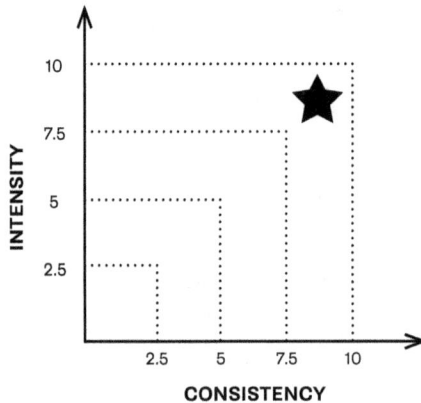

The problem lies in the fact that when we get a bit older, our bodies can't take the intensity anymore. If we keep the intensity high, our consistency will drop as we need more and more time to recover. I have older students who come in and do a super hard workout, but then I won't see them for a week or two. This invariably leads to quitting altogether as they either find it too hard on the body or get down on themselves for being unable to do what they used to do.

On this graph, you can see that with high intensity but low consistency, the person is clearly unhappy!

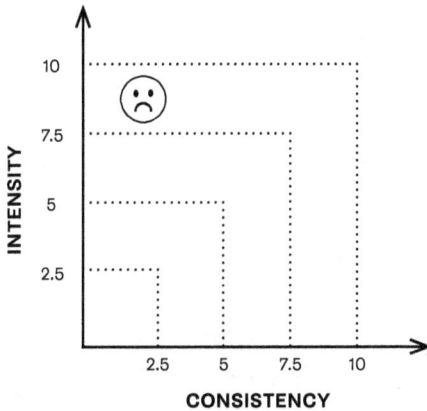

So, we need to give ourselves permission to ease up on the throttle so that we can maintain our consistency, which, of course, as we all know, is the key to growth. Here is what that graph looks like. (Look how happy he is!)

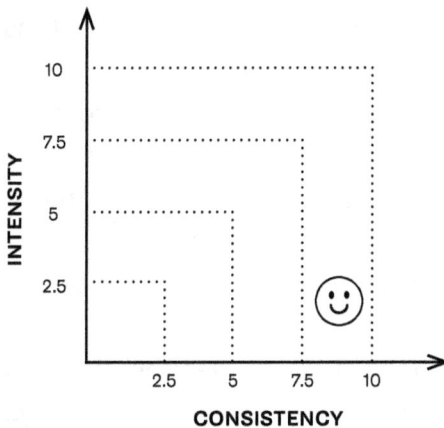

The moral of the story is if you love it, keep going no matter what, if you have to drop the intensity, so be it. You're getting older and that's just fine!

COACHING

One of the best pieces of advice I ever received came from my coach, Ron Balicki. I remember it as if it were yesterday. At the time, I was 23 years old and working as a door supervisor, teaching martial arts, and participating in a few competitions along the way.

That day, I was leaving a heavy training session to pick him up at the airport. When I arrived, he saw my face, which was a bit battered from training with the other doorman, and said, "Matt, you have to learn how to coach. Working on the door is a dead-end job. There are only three ways out of it: hospital, morgue, or jail." He went on to say, "Fighting is a really, really, really hard way to make a living, but if you learn to coach, you can make a career out of it forever."

I am grateful for those words every day! They have probably prolonged my martial arts career by a few decades. They also inspired me to learn everything I could about martial arts so I could pass my passion on to others.

If I'm honest, I suppose my desire to coach is quite selfish. It makes me feel incredibly good to help people become better people and achieve their goals. I still think there is no greater human endeavour than helping others without the thought of reward. Coincidentally, it's one of the best feelings in the world, too!

I sincerely hope that you get the chance to coach one day and pass your knowledge on to others. If you are already a coach, well done; you are changing people's lives, and you should be proud!

NOTES ON AGEING IN MARTIAL ARTS:

- **Martial arts is a journey that reveals its real benefits after five, ten, 20, even 50 years, so stick with it!**

- **Train in short, middle and long term training to extend your lifespan in martial arts.**

- **There will come a time when you can't do what you used to be able to. That's okay; adapt your training to suit you.**

- **Mastery is 10,000 hours or 36,000,000 seconds. Get training!**

- **Knowledge is powerful. Gather it in and pass it on to those who need it. Even if your body is failing you can use what you have learned to help others. It is your legacy!**

CONCLUSION

In one of my fights many years ago, I was getting my butt kicked. I slumped onto my stool in between rounds and pleaded for some advice. "Just fight better" was my cornerman's jokingly helpful advice. "Thanks a lot," I replied.

I guess that is what we all want to do. We just want to fight better. We dedicate ourselves to our coaches and our styles. We scour the Internet and old VHS videos for clues on how to improve.

That's why I wrote this book. I wanted to give you some ideas on how to be a better fighter or martial artist. I wanted to share my journey and discoveries with you so you can take them and run with them. I want you to become the best you can be.

I hope you found something useful in these pages that you can put into practice. If not, this book will make excellent kindling on your next family camping trip!

Being a martial artist is a tough road. You get punched in the face and kicked in the leg when you practise. In order to get better, you have air squeezed from your body and your limbs twisted in ways they weren't meant to be. You sweat for it. You cry for it. You bleed for it. You get kicked in the groin and poked in the eye for it. But it's worth it. It's worth becoming a better fighter because when you do, you truly believe in your value as a human being.

I wish you all the very best in your training, and remember, just fight better!

Matthew Teasdale
Team Phoenix Martial Arts, 2025

ACKNOWLEDGEMENTS

I am incredibly grateful for all of the wonderful people I have met in martial arts. You have inspired me to always be open-minded, research as much as possible, and question everything I do. You have taught me that self-analysis is the key to growth.

I have been with my coach, Ron Balicki, since 1994. When I met Ron, I was just a 15-year-old boy, and yet he took the time to introduce me to an incredible world that I knew nothing about. This world would come to define my whole adult life, and I will be eternally grateful for his kindness, patience and guidance.

His organisation, Martial Arts Research Systems, was founded on the principles of researching and experiencing different martial arts and training methods.

I feel now that the ultimate goal of this training method is to understand the similarities rather than the differences between the arts, for it is in the similarities that we find unity, community, togetherness, and a purpose greater than ourselves.

My coach, Johan Skalberg, inspired me to push myself to improve in every way. His physical approach to training forged my mind and body to handle just about anything the world can throw at me. His teachings on personal leadership and coaching shaped much of what I practise today, and I am forever grateful.

I would also like to say a massive thank you to my coaches, Richard Smith, Rungchai Makete, and Koa Lan Lek, for sharing their incredible knowledge of Muay Thai and Muay Boran with me. These men's dedication to their art is inspiring.

I have been privileged to train with so many amazing coaches over the years. I am lucky to have been in the same room as these people. Thank you very much to Dianna Lee Inosanto, Dan Inosanto, Paul Pearson, Jeff Espinous, Liam Harrison,

Andy Howson, Jordan Watson, Greg LeBoeuf, Paul Vunak, Nokweed Davy, Karl Tanswell, Richard Bustillo, Larry Hartsell, Alain Sailly, Carlos Newton, Royce Gracie, Rickson Gracie, Eric Paulson, Andy Gibney, Danny Guba, Andy Thrasher, Mo Teague, Charles Gossens, Krishna Godhania, Tony Blauer, Eddie Bravo, Keith Florian, Kenny Florian, Chanoi, and many more.

You are nothing if you don't have someone to share it with. This is certainly true with martial arts. You can never hope to become your best if you don't have a good training partner. I want to thank all of my training partners over the years for your commitment and sacrifice in helping me become the best I could be. I hope I was of help to you in your growth as well. Most notably, I would like to thank Simon English, Dan Rizzuto, Iain Brownlee, Adam Dollery, Flavio Ruiz Van Hoof, Brian Watson, Ben Creighton, and Rachel Teasdale. Without these guys, I would still be an apprentice butcher with my head stuck in a pig!

A massive thank you to Sharron Rowntree and Nik Chapman. They are my partners in crime at Team Phoenix and have stuck with me on this exciting journey.

I must give a huge thank you to everyone who helped me put this book together. Without you, it would just be a collection of below-average stickmen! I want you to know how grateful I am for your reading and re-reading, editing, ideas, and contributions. Thanks to Rachel Teasdale, Peter Teasdale, Jason Steggles, James Kyne, Barry Gallacher, and Chris Monks.

Again, thank you to Dr Barry Gallacher for his patience and tireless effort in explaining physics to me. His contribution to this book and to my knowledge of how martial arts works is out of this world.

I want to give a special mention to Chris Monks, whose mentoring on the art of writing was invaluable. He went above and beyond for me, and I really appreciate his help!

It's fascinating and humbling to see a true professional like him at work.

To my students, I want to say that without you, there is no me. You make me want to be better every day, and I learn more from you than you can imagine. I especially want to thank those who have stuck with me for a decade or more. I know you have had to put up with a lot, and I certainly appreciate your dedication!

The final thank you goes to my family. To my mother and stepfather, Lennie and Mike, and my father and stepmother, Peter and Shelley, I want to thank you for shaping me into the person I have become. I'm not perfect, but you let me know that being imperfect is okay. I can't even imagine how it must feel when your teenage child wants to drop out of school and become a martial arts coach! Thank you for your patience and understanding of my dream.

Thank you so much to my step-siblings, Mark and Marsha, who always told me to do what I believed in. Following your passion is difficult, and you need people encouraging you to keep going. Thank you both.

To my UK family, I want to say a huge thank you for their acceptance, love and encouragement over the years. Their support is worth more than gold. Thank you to Bex, James, Harry, Pav, Doreen, Scott, Pam, Keith, Mary, Tommy, Yvonne, Tom, Vic, Chris, Steph, Gemma, Kinga and all the rest of the family.

I want to thank my grandparents Pat and Alan Greaves for their love and affection as I was growing up. I truly wish I could show you how far I have come. To my grandparents Joan and Vivian Teasdale, I have to say that this dream would not have been possible without you. Thank you for all of your unrelenting support over the years. I will keep doing my best to make you proud.

Finally, thank you to my wonderful wife, Rachel. I don't even know how to start thanking her. To put up with me on a day-to-day basis takes incredible patience. Thank you for putting up with the daily requests to punch or kick me and letting me try new techniques on you. Thank you for listening to me prattle on endlessly about every martial arts topic fathomable. Most of all, thank you for believing in me. Without your love and support, none of this would have been possible. You are an amazing person. I love you.

Thank You!

Matthew Teasdale is a life-long martial artist and coach. His passion for the martial arts was ignited in 1992 when his mother took him to his very first Tae kwon do class. Since then, he has followed his dream of training and teaching martial arts around the world. Matthew holds Instructor qualifications in MARS Kali, Kali Sikaran International, Jeet Kune Do / Jun Fan, MARS Grappling, and Muay Thai. Matthew is the Owner and Head coach of Team Phoenix Martial Arts in Newcastle upon Tyne, UK and has had the privilege of working with thousands of students there since 2002.

www.ingramcontent.com/pod-product-compliance
Lightning Source LLC
Chambersburg PA
CBHW062102080426
42734CB00012B/2720